Windows 95

Jim Muir

Senior Lecturer in Business Computing at
Bournemouth University.

Letts
1996

acknowledgments

'Windows^{TM} 95 ^{TM} Screen Shots © 1995 Microsoft Corporation. All rights reserved, reprinted with permission from Microsoft Corporation.'

A CIP record for this book is available from the British Library.

ISBN 1 85805 124 X

Reprinted 1998

Typeset by KAI, Nottingham, UK

Printed in Great Britain by Ashford Colour Press, Gosport.

contents

introduction

aims

This book is intended for any new user of Windows 95. It provides a clear and practical guide to making effective use of Windows 95. The book assumes no technical knowledge and is suitable for use at college, work or home.

structure

The book introduces the features of Windows 95 in the context of practical activities to perform or problems to solve. In this way any underlying theory is supported with opportunities for independent practice and consolidation.

There are nine units, each of which has the following features:

- Short activities which guide the user step-by-step through the necessary skills
- Consolidation activities to be completed with minimal support from the book
- A trouble-shooting section after each activity with advice on what to do if a command doesn't work

At the end of the book there are solutions to selected activities to help check on progress.

a note to lecturers and students

This learning material requires little, if any, input by lecturers, and can therefore be used on programmes based on independent learning. A disk containing the files used in the book is available free to all lecturers adopting the book as a course text.

what is an operating system, and what is Windows 95?

At this stage a theoretical definition of an operating system would probably be confusing and unhelpful. However, it is important to realise very early on that the operating system is the software or set of programs which controls the basic actions of your hardware – the keyboard, screen, main memory, disk drive and so on. In addition, the operating system loads and runs application software and manages your data files. It might be helpful to think of the operating system as a bridge between you, your hardware and your programs. It translates your commands into a form that the computer can understand so that you can use the software to do the job you bought it for. And without you realising it, the operating system is working in the background on utility or housekeeping programs: copying or deleting files on disk, backing up the whole disk or checking the hardware.

Windows 95 is the latest operating system developed by Microsoft. It is not the only operating system but it is becoming the standard system used on most PCs. This degree of standardisation is of great benefit as it allows software applications to be developed which will run on most PCs.

Conventions used

The terms 'DOS' and 'MS-DOS' are used interchangeably.

The terms 'PC', 'personal computer' and 'computer' are used interchangeably.

Keyboard entries may be typed in lower or upper case. I use upper case for clarity. If you wish to use upper case then use the Caps Lock key.

Diskettes needed

For these activities you will need two suitable three and a half inch high density diskettes, (floppy disks) preferably new ones that do not contain any files. The Format and Delete commands will erase any information on them.

A brand new disk needs to be formatted before it can be used – consult Unit 3, Activity 1 for information on different disk formats if necessary.

New features of Windows 95

Microsoft released Windows 95 in August 1995. It offers the first major re-design of Windows since its launch in the 1980's. All the standard elements of the Graphical User Interface are still present – windows, mouse, icons, pull-down menus etc – but they have been radically redesigned. There are also changes 'behind the scenes' that are not so immediately apparent. These are briefly explained below, but may not mean much to you unless you are already familiar with MS-DOS and/or Windows. Some of the major new features are:

MS-DOS no longer needed: Windows 95 no longer requires the MS-DOS operating system in order to run; it is a complete operating system in its own right and able to run older DOS and Windows programs. Your PC may still have MS-DOS installed to maintain compatibility with older MS-DOS-based programs.

Microsoft term Windows 95 a 'pre-emptive multithreading, multitasking operating system' *Multitasking* means that more than one program or application can run at once (as they could in Windows 3.1) *pre-emptive multithreading* means very simply that different sections or threads of different programs can be run at the same time, thereby improving processing speed.

Longer file names: File names can be up to 255 characters long. Previously the limit was 8 characters followed by an optional extension of up to 3 characters.

The Start Button and Task Bar: The Start button provides a single starting point for all Windows Features. The Task bar indicates which applications are running. They avoid the need to have multiple windows open, as was sometimes the case with earlier versions of Windows.

Support for networks: If you are connected to a network the built in networking features make it easier to communicate with other computers and share files.

Finding files and running programs. The Find and Quick View commands make it easier to search for and locate a file, the Run command speeds up running a program.

Customising Windows. There are various ways to tailor Windows to individual needs – shortcuts to applications, setting up different user profiles and altering how applications run.

New and improved features. An improved built-in word processor and paint program are provided, the file display and backup are also improved. New features include fax, electronic mail, a phone dialler, and a disk compressor and defragmenter.

Plug and play. This is an industry-wide standard; Windows 95 will automatically detect when new peripherals such as disk drives, adapters, CD-ROMs, and sound cards are plugged in and reconfigure the PC to manage the new component. The devices can be 'played' straight away without the user needing to go through complex set up routines.

If you already know Windows 3.1

Many readers will already be familiar with Windows 3.1 or Windows for Workgroups, the previous versions of Windows. You will find using Windows 95 fairly straightforward, though initially you will miss such familiar features as File Manager, Program Manager, and the Main group windows. To help you find your way around, brief notes, labelled as follows:

3.1 ⇨ 95

The difference between the two ....

explain the differences between new and old versions.

unit 1

Windows 95 – the introductory essentials

Introduction

In this unit you will learn such essential preliminaries as starting up Windows, finding your way around the desktop and Task Bar, opening and closing windows and using Help. Don't be tempted to skip these activities if you are fairly new to Windows. They lay the foundation for more advanced skills and they give you a general understanding of what Windows is and how it works.

Skills covered	Activity
Control-menu box – using	3.13
Dialogue box – using	4.2
Help – using	4
icons – rearranging	3.14
Menus – using	3.8
Mouse actions	2.5
Scrolling	2.4, 4.9
Window – closing	2.2, 3.13
Window – opening	1.3
Window features – using	1
Window – maximising	1.3, 2.1, 3.12
Window – minimising	1.3, 2.1, 3.12
Window – restoring	1.3, 2.1
Window size – changing	2.3
Windows – arranging	3

Previous skills required

None

Activity 1 The Windows 95 opening screen

Windows is a Graphical User Interface (GUI). This means that you use graphical or picture-based methods to carry out operations on your computer.

1. When you turn on your PC you are taken directly to the Windows desktop. Let's identify the basic components first. They are labelled on Figure 1 – don't worry if yours differ from this.

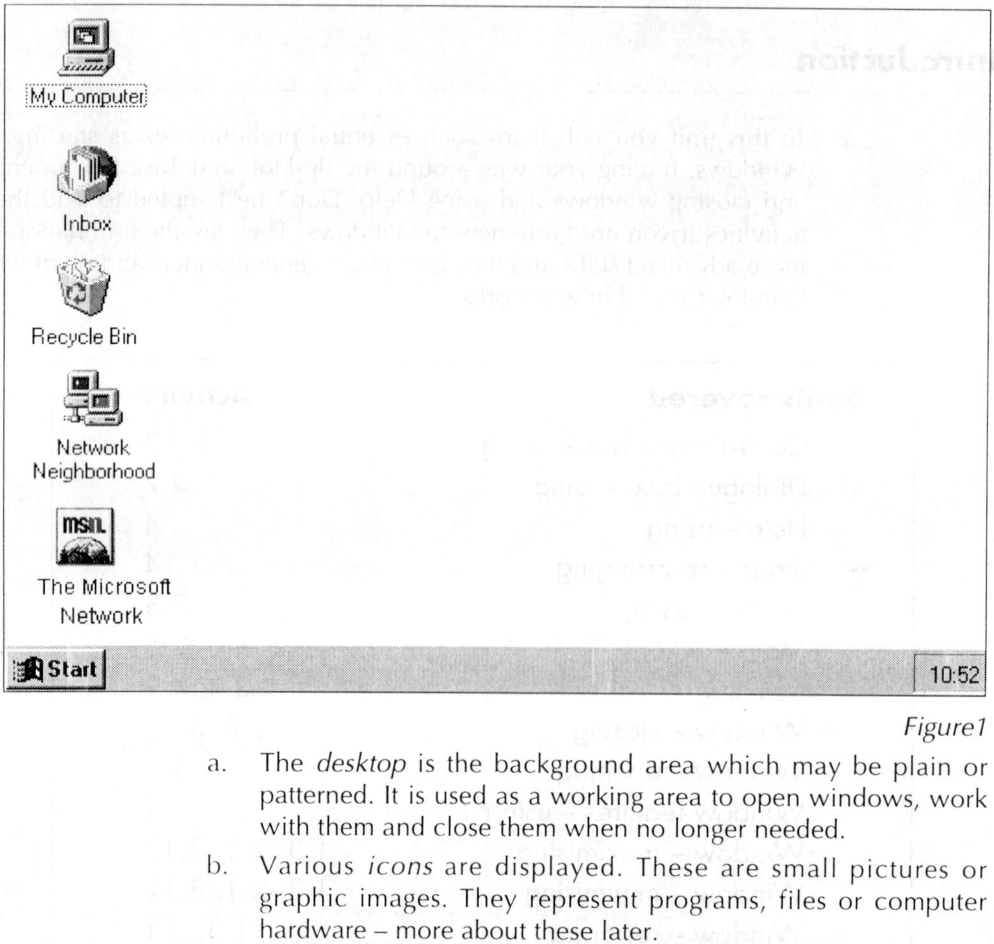

Figure1

a. The *desktop* is the background area which may be plain or patterned. It is used as a working area to open windows, work with them and close them when no longer needed.

b. Various *icons* are displayed. These are small pictures or graphic images. They represent programs, files or computer hardware – more about these later.

c. The *taskbar* is displayed along the bottom of the screen. If you are not using any program or file then it will only display the Start button and the time – see Figure 1 above.

3.1 ⇨ 95

> All the standard windows of Windows 3.1 – Main, Program Manager, File Manager etc – have been replaced. Don't worry, you can achieve the same tasks as simply in Windows 95. This unit will show you the standard menus and your Windows 3.1 experience can be applied.

2. Troubleshooting.

If someone has been using the computer before you you may find the opening screen is overlaid by some other windows or the Welcome Screen. If so proceed as follows.

Move the mouse – the pointer on the screen moves. In the top right hand corner of the open window are 3 small icons. Move the pointer onto the one marked with a cross and press the left hand button of the mouse. The window will close.

If one icon is laying on top of another move the mouse on top of the icon, press down the left mouse button and move the mouse to drag it away.

3. Now move the screen pointer onto the **My Computer** icon. It may have been re-named, if so identify it by the icon – a picture of a PC.

Press the left button on the mouse twice in quick succession. The icon opens up into a window – try again if it doesn't work.

A window is simply a rectangular area that displays further information – icons, folders or files. At the moment it shows details of the PC's resources – disk drives, printers etc.

3.1 ⇨ 95

> The My Computer window also contains the Control Panel. You can use it to work with files and drives, eg view, sort, copy, rename and delete files.

We will use the My Computer window to identify the main components of a window and try some of them out. Keep referring to Figure 2 if necessary. Again don't worry if your window is different to the one shown.

a. **The Control-menu icon** is in the top left-hand corner of every window. The icon varies, depending on the application.
   It allows you to close, move and alter the sizes of windows.

b. **Title and title bar.** Every window has these. Depending on the type of window the title can be the name of an application (program), a file or, as in the case of My Computer, a group of resources. If there are several windows open then the title bar of the *active* window – the one that you are using – appears as a deeper colour than the others

c. **The Menu Bar** appears just below the Title Bar and shows a list of options – File, Options, View and Help. Each menu option contains a list of related commands, the menu options will vary from one window to another.
Using a menu is the main method of issuing commands and involves two steps, selecting the menu option then choosing a command from it.

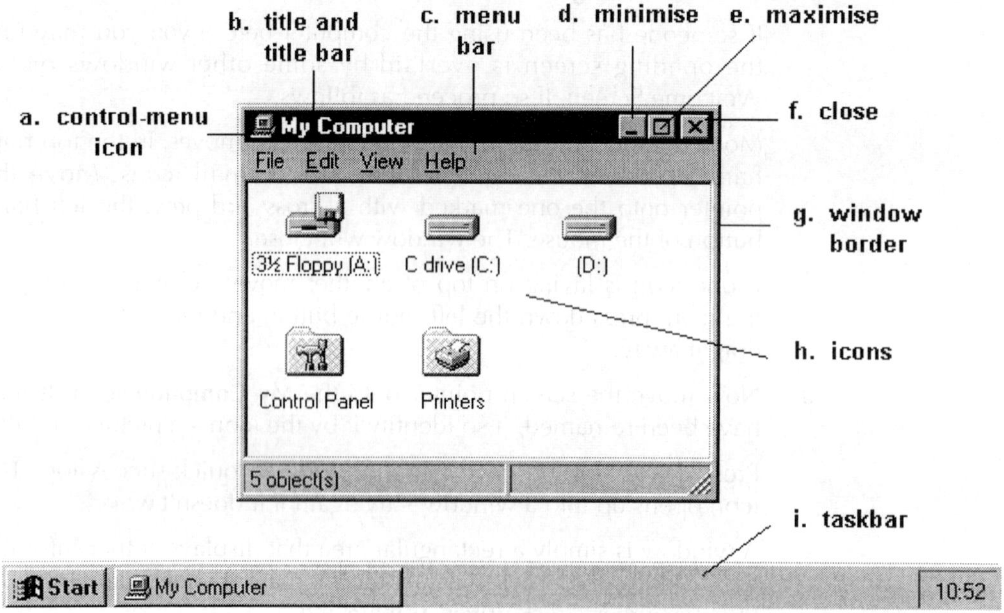

Figure 2

d. **The Minimise Button** is in the top right hand corner of every window. It allows you to reduce the window to a button on the taskbar. This is useful and you will be using it later.

e. **The Maximise Button** (immediately to the right of the Minimise button) allows you to enlarge the window to the full size of the screen. This gives you more room to work if needed. If the screen is already maximised then the Maximise button is replaced by a double-squared Restore button that restores the window to its previous size.

f. The **Close** Button is used when you no longer need a window, eg you have finished using an application.

g. **The Window Border** is a line enclosing each window. The sides and corners of the border can be used to change the size of a window.

h. **Icons** represent Windows which aren't being used at the moment- the picture on each of them indicates that they contain further groups of applications that are currently inactive.

i. **The Taskbar** is always visible while Windows 95 is running. It shows the Start button, plus a button for every task you have started, eg program running or document open. So in Figure 2 the taskbar shows the Start button and a button for **My Computer** indicating that this task is running.

The open My Computer window also shows a taskbar reporting '5 objects', ie 5 items in this window.

3.1 ⇨ 95

> You will recognise these standard Windows features; the main changes are the addition of a close button, plus minimised windows being displayed on the taskbar as buttons.

Activity 2 Re-sizing and closing windows

Now that we've identified some of the basic Windows components, let's try some of them out; keep referring to Figure 2 if necessary.

1. **Maximising and minimising windows**. This often causes frustration when you start out; typical problems are a window suddenly enlarging, shrinking, disappearing or overlaying another.

   Make sure that the **My Computer** window is still open.

   Move the screen pointer onto the **maximise** button and click once. The window enlarges to fill the whole screen and the maximise button is replaced by the **restore** button.

   Click the **restore** button and the window assumes its previous size.

   Now click the **minimise** button. The My Computer Window shrinks to a button on the taskbar as the application is still running as a 'task'.

   Click the button on the taskbar and the My Computer window opens again.

2. **Closing windows.** Click the **close** button. The window is completely closed – there is no button on the Taskbar as the application is no longer running.

   Open it again by moving the screen pointer onto the My Computer icon and double-clicking.

3. **Window size.**To make finer adjustments we must use the window border. You cannot do this while the window is maximised so click the restore button if necessary.

Move the screen pointer to the bottom right-hand border of the window – the screen pointer changes to a double-headed arrow when correctly located.
Now press down the left mouse button *and keep it pressed down.*

Drag the mouse so that the edge of the worksheet moves diagonally towards the top left of the screen. Release the button when the My Computer window measures about 2 inches square.

Your Window will now resemble Figure 3.

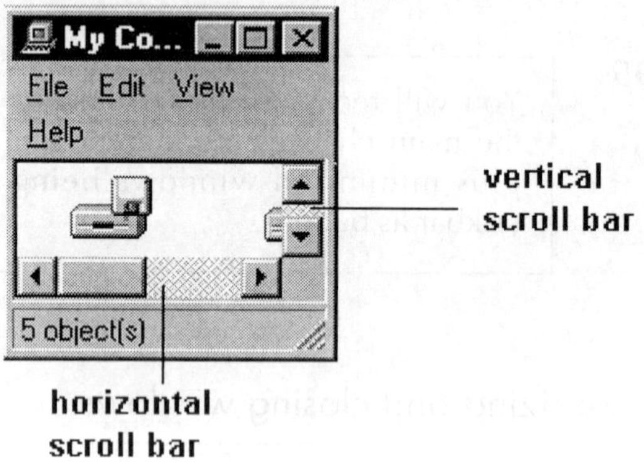

Figure 3

Three main changes have taken place:

First the Title and Menu Bars are much shortened – the four menu options may have 'wrapped round' in order to fit them in, secondly some or all of the icons seem to have disappeared – compare the re-sized Window with Figure 2.

Thirdly two new Windows features have appeared – horizontal and vertical scroll bars. if you don't have both sets of scroll bars then make the window even smaller until they appear.

Scroll bars are permanent features of some windows, but with windows such as My Computer they will only appear if the window is too small to show all the icons.

4. **Scrolling.** Move the screen pointer onto the down arrow button of the vertical scroll bar and hold the mouse button down. The window scrolls, revealing some of the concealed icons

   Now move the screen pointer onto the left and right arrow buttons of the horizontal scroll bar and hold down the mouse button as before, the rest of the icons scroll into view.

   Finally restore the window to its previous size – drag the border of the window diagonally to the bottom right of the screen.
   All the icons will be in view again. If so the scroll bars will have disappeared – they are not needed.

5. **Mouse control.** You have now learnt 3 of the 4 basic mouse actions:

Clicking – locate screen pointer, press left mouse button once

Double clicking – locate screen pointer and press left mouse button twice in quick succession

Dragging – locate screen pointer, hold down left button while moving the mouse, release button.

Right click – locate screen pointer, press right mouse button once. When you click an object with the right mouse button it either opens up a *context* menu letting you perform actions on the object or lets you get further information about it. You will be using right click in the next activity.

From now on I shall be using these names to refer to these actions.

Activity 3 Working with multiple windows

Confusion often arises when you have more than one Window open at once; try out the following tasks.

1. If you are starting a new Windows session make sure that only the My Computer Window is open – see Activity 2 above.
2. Enlarge the size of the window and use the scroll bars if necessary so that all the icons are visible- see Activity 2 above.
3. Now move the screen pointer onto the **Control Panel** icon and double click. The window opens, overlaying the My Computer window.
   A further group of icons are displayed in this second window, representing further applications. Two buttons are displayed on the Taskbar, indicating applications that are running.

   Your screen should resemble Figure 4. Don't worry if the relative positions and sizes of your two windows vary from this.
4. Now double-click the **Fonts** icon in the Control Panel window – a third window is now opened.

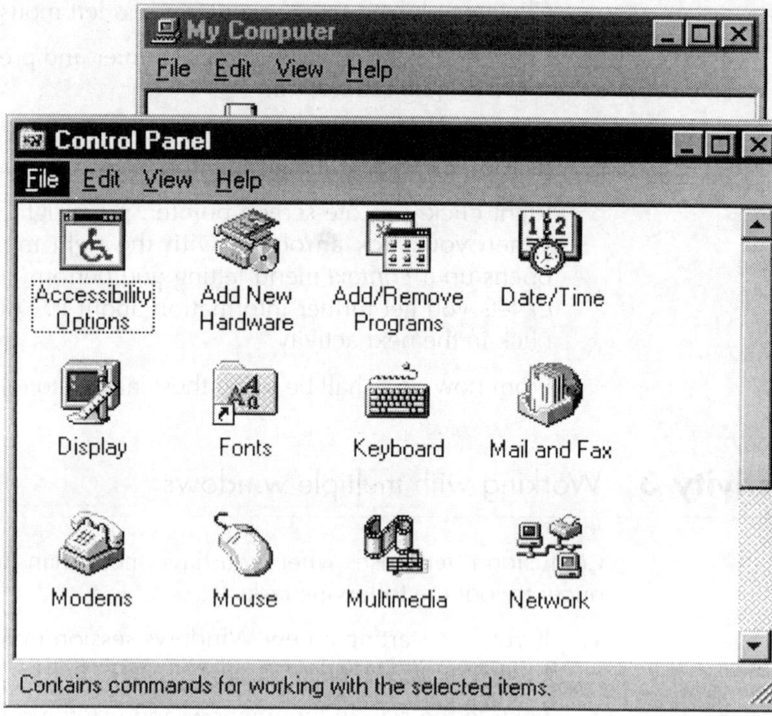

Figure 4

5. **Troubleshooting.** If you can only see one window first check the task bar, it should show 3 tasks – My Computer, Control Panel and Fonts

6. It is now easy to see how working with multiple windows can cause confusion; one window overlays another, often hiding the title and the icons it contains. Let's experiment with moving and re-sizing these windows.

7. For the purposes of the exercises that follow we will need to make each window fairly small so that they overlay each other. Re-size them (see Activity 2) so that they resemble Figure 5. It doesn't matter which window is on top for the moment.

8. **Using Menus.** We can re-arrange the windows on the desktop.

   Move the screen pointer onto a blank area on the task bar (ie not on a task button)

   Right click – a shortcut menu opens revealing a number of options – see Figure 6.

   Shortcut keys: You will notice that a letter is underlined in each menu option, eg Cascade, Tile Horizontally etc. This allows commands to be issued from the keyboard, rather than using a mouse. If you hold down the Alt or Ctrl key and type the appropriate letter the command is executed.

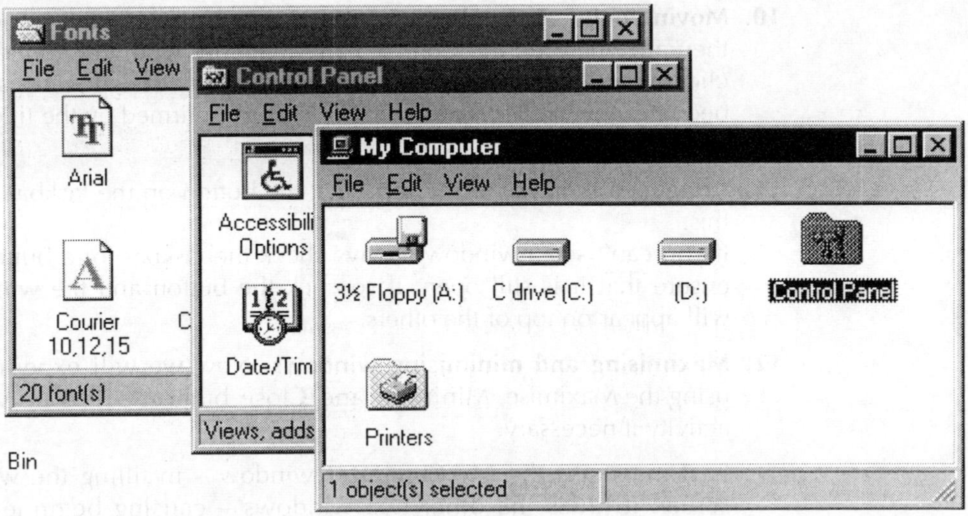

Figure 5

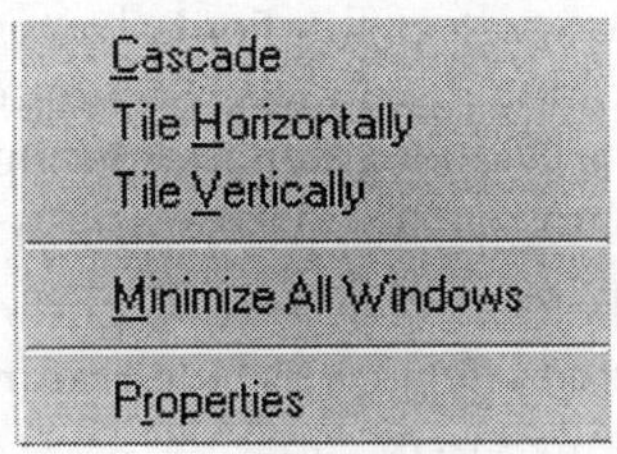

Figure 6

In these units we will be using the mouse, not the keyboard equivalent.

9. **Moving and arranging windows**. Move the screen pointer onto the menu option **Tile horizontally** and click.
The command is executed and the icons are arranged side by side on the desktop.

Open the menu again and this time choose the option **Cascade.**
This command displays the windows so that they overlap, keeping the window titles visible.

Now try the third option – **Tile vertically.**

Now drag the three windows to new positions – place the screen pointer on the Title Bar of each window, click it to select it, then drag.
Repeat the **Tile** commands and the windows are re-arranged as before.

Finally select the **Cascade** option.

10. **Moving between windows.** Click anywhere on the **Fonts** window, then anywhere on the **Control Panel** window. You will notice that clicking a window selects it so that it overlays the other ones and becomes the 'active' window. This is also confirmed by the title bar changing colour.

11. **Bringing a window to the top**.Click the button on the taskbar – try this.
    If you can't see a window always check the taskbar for a button to ensure that it is still open, if so click the button and the window will appear on top of the others.

12. **Maximising and minimising windows.** Now we will experiment using the Maximise, Minimise and Close buttons – see previous activity if necessary.

    First maximise the **My Computer** window – in filling the whole screen it hides the other two windows – causing beginners to wonder where they have gone!

    Now select the **Fonts** button on the task bar – it overlays the My Computer window. Minimise the **My Computer** window.
    The window seems to disappear altogether; in fact it has become a button on the taskbar as it is still running.

    Click on the **My Computer** button – the window fills the whole screen again – use the **restore** button to return it to its previous size.

    Right click a blank area of the task bar – the menu appears as before.
    This time select the option **Minimise all windows** – they are all reduced to buttons on the taskbar.

13. **Closing windows.** Click on the three buttons to open the windows again.
    The three windows that we are using are group windows – they contain further groups of icons rather than being applications in their own right.

    Close the topmost window using the close button – it no longer appears on the taskbar as a button.

    We can also close a window using the Control-menu box in the top left hand corner of the window – see Figure 1 above. This can be useful if other parts of the window are hidden.
    Click the Control-menu box on another window and a menu is opened – see Figure 7.

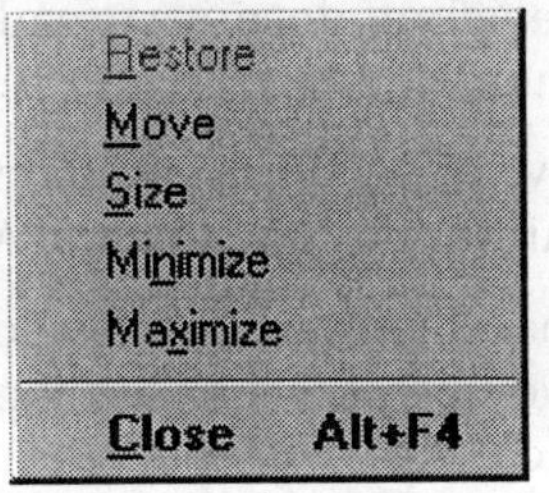

Figure 7

The top group of options duplicate ones we have already learnt.

Click the **Close** option and the active window is closed.

Repeat for any windows remaining open. (Hint: double clicking the Control-menu icon closes the window in one operation)

14. Re-arranging icons. You will have noticed that making windows smaller means that some of the icons disappear from view.

Open the **My Computer** window.

Move the screen pointer onto the menu bar and click the word **View** – the **View** menu opens.

Click the **Arrange Icons** option to select it – a second menu opens.

Make sure that the **Auto Arrange** option is off, ie if it is ticked then click it to de-select the option.

Note: This command is an examples of a switch option – it can be set on or off by clicking it, 'on' being indicated by a tick or check mark next to the option.

15. Now alter the size of the window so it resembles Figure 8. The presence of scroll bars tell you that there are icons currently not in view.

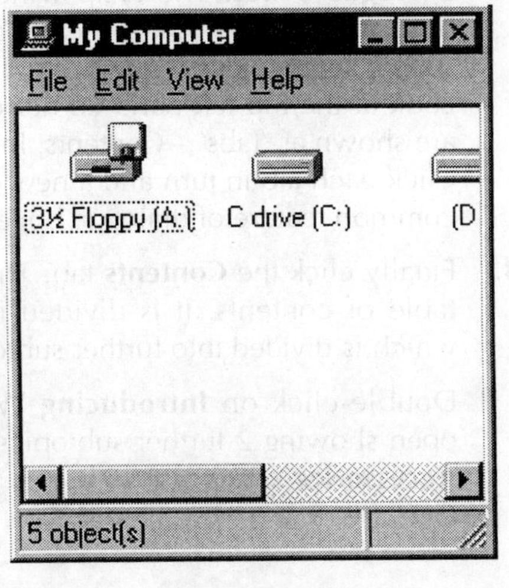

Figure 8

The icons do not spread out to fill the available space in the window.

Now open the **View** menu and select the **Arrange Icons** option again. Make sure that the **Auto Arrange** option is on, ie it is ticked.

When the Auto Arrange command is turned on then any icons that have been compressed together will spread out to fill the available space.

3.1 ➪ 95

> Minimised (but not closed) windows appear as buttons on the taskbar. This makes it easier to open a minimised window – in Windows 3.1 a minimised window icon was often hidden by an open window.

Activity 4 Using Help

Windows offers good help and tutorial facilities on basic commands, operations,concepts and technical information. There are two main ways to start Help:

Main desktop – Click the Start button on the taskbar then click Help.

From a window – Click the Help option on the menu bar.

Either way will take you to the same list of topics.

1. Click the **Start** button on the task bar. A menu appears.

   Click the **Help** option. A dialogue box appears showing the list of help topics.

2. **Dialogue boxes.** The Help window is an example of a *dialogue* box. A dialogue box either contains a message or asks you to supply some information.
   Look at the top left hand corner of the dialogue box, three choices are shown as 'tabs' – Contents, Index and Find.
   Click each tab in turn and a new dialogue box is shown – tabs are a common feature of dialogue boxes.

3. Finally click the **Contents** tab. The Contents feature is like a book's table of contents. It is divided into topics or 'chapters', each of which is divided into further subtopics.

   Double-click on **Introducing Windows** – the book icon is now open showing 2 further subtopics – **Welcome** and **Using Windows Accessories** – see Figure 9.

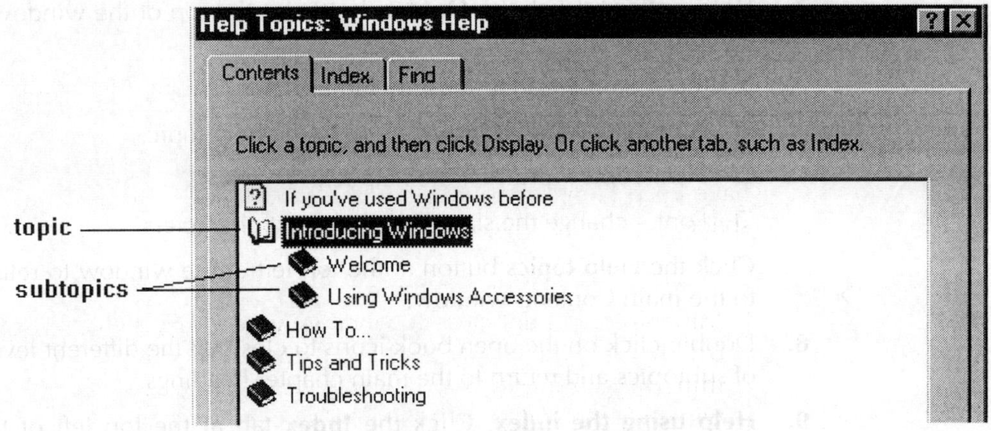

Figure 9

4. Double click on the **Welcome** icon and a further list of subtopics is displayed – you can tell the levels by the indentation of the icons.

5. Next click the topic **A list of what's new**

   Now that you have reached the third level help 'pages' are offered, marked with question mark icons – see Figure 10.

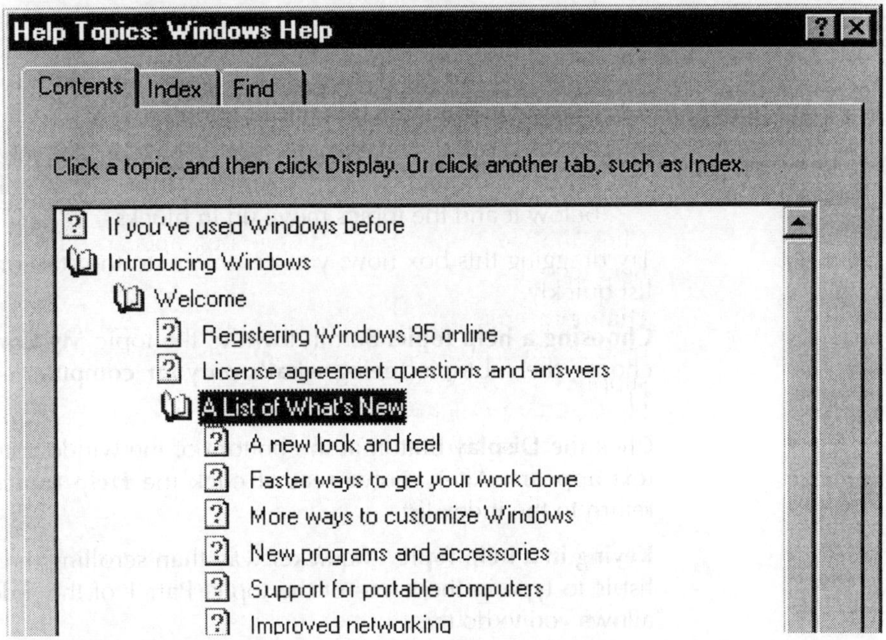

Figure 10

6. Double click the option **A new look and feel**.
   Further choices are offered in a new window. Take time to review a few of these – you don't need to close the help window when you go from topic to topic – only when you have finished reading the list.

7. **Help options**. Click the **Options** button at the top of the window – a menu appears.

   It offers a number of options, including:

   ❒ Annotate – add your own notes to the help topic.

   ❒ Print Topic – print off the help text.

   ❒ Font – change the size of the help text characters.

   Click the **Help topics** button at the top left of the window to return to the main Contents window.

8. Double click on the open book icons to close up the different levels of subtopics and return to the main chapter headings.

9. **Help using the index**. Click the **Index** tab at the top left of the window. All the help topics are listed alphabetically. Provided you are fairly sure of your topic this feature can be quicker to use than negotiating several levels of contents as we have just done.

   Let's view the index topics, we can take this opportunity to try out different scrolling techniques :

   a. **Slow scrolling.** Position the screen pointer on the up or down arrow on the scroll bar and click once – the text scrolls line by line.

   b. **Continuous scrolling.** Position the screen pointer on the up or down arrow on the scroll bar and keep the mouse button pressed down – the text scrolls continuously

   c. **Rapid scrolling.** Identify the scroll box on the scroll bar – its position indicates your position in the list. Click above or below it and the topics move up in blocks.

   Try dragging this box now; you can move to the start or end of the list quickly.

   Choosing a help topic. Scroll down to the topic **My Computer** and choose the subtopic **seeing what's on your computer** – see Figure 11.

   Click the **Display** button at the bottom of the window and the help text appears. After you've read it click the **Help topics** button to return to the index list.

   Keying in a help topic. A quicker way than scrolling through a long list is to type in the name of the topic. Part 1 of the index window allows you to do this.

   Move your cursor to the start of the text in box 1 and if necessary drag to highlight the text that it contains – see Figure 11 below. Now type in the three letters **tas** – the index moves to this section of topics.

   Find **Taskbar** and choose the subtopic **minimising windows**.

   Click the **Help topics** button to return to the index list.

Finally click the **Cancel** button to exit help.

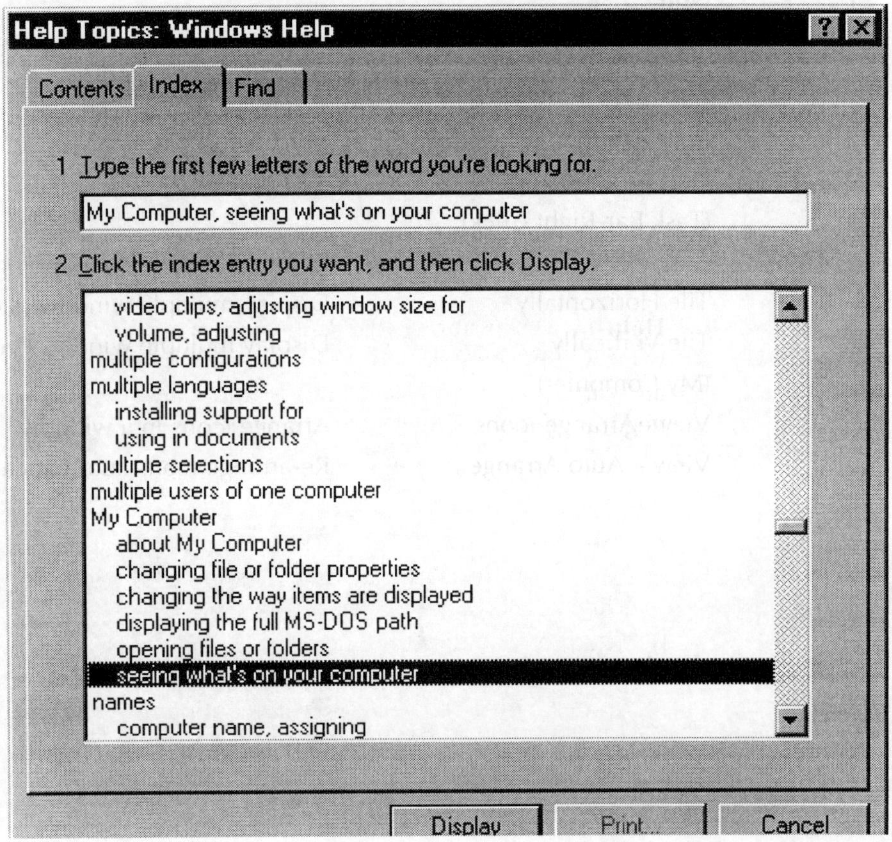

Figure 11

10. Independent activity. Use the Help **Contents** feature to locate help on the following:

- Tips and Tricks – Tip of the Day
- How to – Use Help
- Use the Help **Index** feature to locate help on the following:
- Screen savers
- Internet – connecting to

Summary of commands

Note

Commands show the object to select first, followed by the command to choose from the menu, e.g. Start Button-Help means click the Start Button and select the Help command. Where a command is available from a particular window this is indicated in brackets.

Start Button-Help	Call up Help
(Task Bar-Right Click)	
Cascade	Display multiple overlapping windows
Tile Horizontally	Display multiple windows side by side
Tile Vertically	Display multiple windows vertically
(My Computer)	
View- Arrange icons	Arrange icons in a window
View – Auto Arrange	Re-arrange icons automatically

unit 2

Applications and files

Introduction

In this unit you will be creating a set of files to use in later activities. You will be using two standard Windows applications, Notepad and Wordpad, to do this. You will also learn how to save different versions of a file under different names and how to view the files you have created on disk.

Skills covered	Activity
Application – exiting	1.10
Application – running	3.2, 5
Calculator – using	3.3
Date – setting	3.5
Disk Drive – selecting	1.4, 4.2
File – renaming	1.7
File – saving	1.4
Files – viewing	4
Multitasking	3.7
Notepad Application – using	1
Start button – using	1
Time – setting	3.5
Wordpad – using	2

Previous skills required	covered in unit
Using the standard Windows components	1

Resources required

A new blank diskette

Activity 1 Running an application from the Start menu

The Start button is always on screen and can be used at any time. It is the gateway to all the essential Windows tasks such as starting programs, finding files, getting help and exiting Windows.

3.1 ⇨ 95

In Windows 3.1 you used Program Manager or group window to run a program. In Windows 95 the Start button offers a menu allowing you various ways to run programs.

Note: You will need a suitable diskette (floppy disk) for this exercise, preferably a new one that does not contain any files.

A brand new disk needs to be formatted before it can be used – consult Unit 3 if necessary.

In this activity we will use the Start menu to run an application. An application is any program (or set of programs) that carries out a particular job, eg accounts, or word processing. We are going to use Notepad as our first example application. It is a text editor, (rather like a very simple word processor) and we will use it to create some short text files.

1. Click the **Start** button – bottom left of the taskbar. A menu opens.

   Move the pointer onto the **Programs** options.
   A further menu opens, move the pointer onto the **Accessories** option and a third menu opens – see Figure 1.

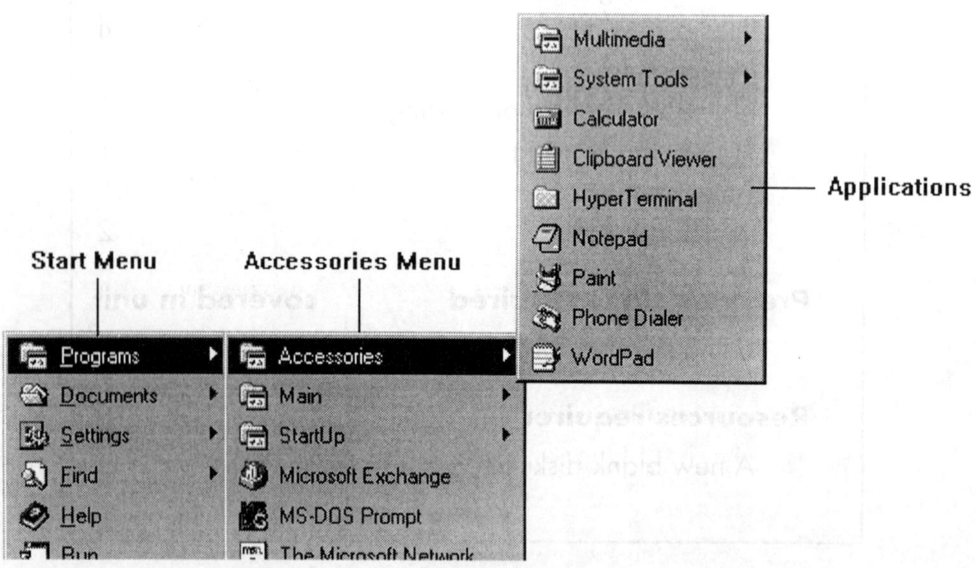

Figure 1

Troubleshooting: If you open the wrong menu click elsewhere on the desktop and start again.

Find the icon labelled **Notepad** and double click it.
The application then loads (ie Windows looks for the application program on the hard disk and loads it into the computer's main memory)

2. A blank notepad window is displayed, waiting for you to enter some text – see Figure 2.

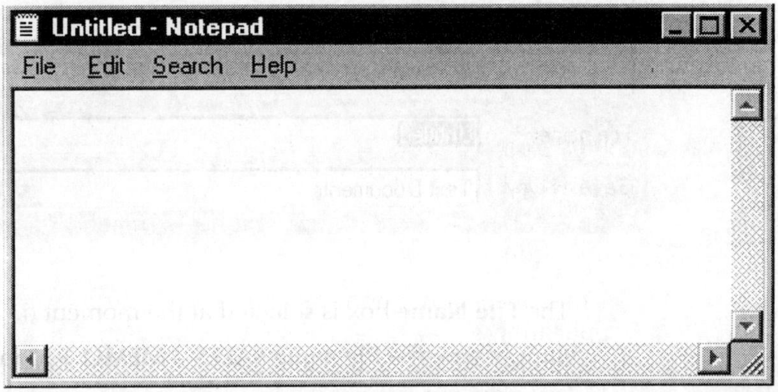

Figure 2

Notice that it contains many standard windows features that you have already used, eg title, menu and scroll bars as well as maximise and minimise buttons.
The flashing bar indicates the insertion point for the text.

3. **Creating text files.** For your future activities in Windows 95 you will need a set of files for you to work with. These can be 'dummy' files, meaning that it doesn't really matter what they contain. However *you must use the file names suggested* as we will be using them in later exercises such as listing, copying, renaming and sorting. So if your typing skills are minimal merely fill them with a jumble of characters. (lecturers using these units as a course text can obtain these files on disk from the publishers – see preface)

   First open the **Edit** menu and select the **Word Wrap** option. This ensures that the when the text that you type reaches the end of the line it 'wraps round' to the next line.

   Simply type in a few lines of text now.

4. **Saving files.** At the moment the text that you have created is only saved in the computer's main memory. The Notepad file has the temporary name 'Untitled' and will be lost as soon as you exit the notebook application unless you save it as a named file.

   Open the **File** menu and choose the **Save As** option. The Save As dialogue box appears next – see Figure 3.

Figure 3

The **File Name** box is selected at the moment (i.e. highlighted)

Simply type the file name **SALES – MEMO 1** (upper or lower case).

Now click the Down Arrow on the **Save in**: box – a list of available drives appears – see Figure 4.

Figure 4

Now select the **3 1/2 Floppy (A:)** option.

In the activities in these units, a diskette will be used to save work. **A:** is your diskette drive; make sure that you have a suitably formatted diskette in A drive. If you are using a brand new diskette it may need formatting – see Unit 3.

Make sure that the **Save as type** box reads **Text Documents.**

Finally click the **Save** button. The command is executed and the file SALES – MEMO 1 is saved to diskette, the drive light comes on to show that the Notepad data is being written (saved) to disk.

If you make a mistake then click the **Cancel** button and start again.

A note on drives. On your PC a hard disk, is used to store Windows and often other applications, e.g. word processor, spreadsheet or database. If you have enough disk space you can also use the hard disk to save work that you create. However it is common to save work on a diskette (also known as a floppy disk) especially where space on the hard disk is limited or if you want to work on more than one computer.

5. The dialogue box disappears and you are returned to the Notepad window which now displays the file name of the newly saved file SALES – MEMO 1 (see the Notes on File Names section at the end of this Activity)

6. **Saving changes.** Add a few more lines of text to this file. These changes will need saving permanently to disk too.

Open the **File** menu; this time choose the **Save** option. (*not Save as*) The drive light comes on again indicates that the changes are being permanently saved to to the SALES – MEMO 1 file on disk.

7. **Saving a file under a new name.** Add a few more lines of text to the file; open the **File** menu again, but now choose the **Save As** option.

The Save As dialogue box appears; amend the file name to **SALES – MEMO 2**

Make sure that the Save in: box still shows **3 1/2 Floppy A:**

Click the **Save** button. The drive light comes on as before to show that the new file SALES – MEMO 2 is being written (saved) to disk.

8. The Notepad window now displays the file name SALES – MEMO 2 – the original file SALES – MEMO 1 is saved and closed and the new copy opened.
Now we'll use this method again to create six more files; first add a few more lines of text (this means that all files will vary slightly in size), then choose Save As from the File menu as before.

Name the files that you create as follows:

SALES – MEMO 3
SALES – MEMO 4
ACCOUNTS – MEMO 1
ACCOUNTS – MEMO 2
ACCOUNTS – MEMO 3
ACCOUNTS – MEMO 4

When you have created these files open the **File** menu and select the **Open** option; your display should resemble Figure 5.

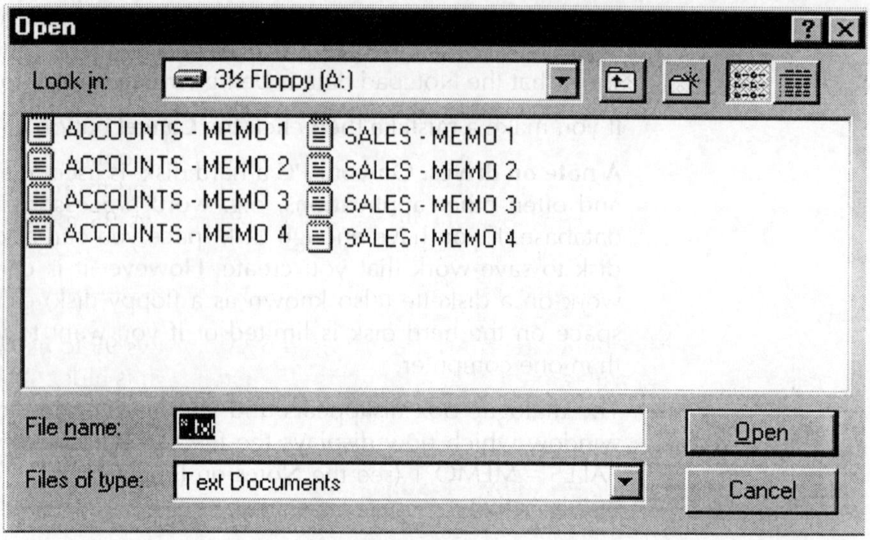

Figure 5

ie 8 text files have been created using the Notepad application.
Click the **Cancel** button on the Open dialogue box.

9. **Note on naming conventions.** The file name starts with the department name – Accounts or Sales – followed by the type of document – memo.
The final number on the file name is the order of creation and ensures that each file name is unique.

   When you are creating files make sure that you use a meaningful, memorable naming convention and stick to it.

10. **Exiting and saving a file.** Add another line to the final file that you have created. Now try to exit the Notepad application as follows; open the **File** menu and select **Exit.** A dialogue box appears, reminding you that you have not saved the changes made to the document. All Windows applications have this feature reminding you to save your work. Normally you would click the Yes button which saves and exits the document.

    Click the **Cancel** button which returns you to the document.

    A situation where you *would* find it useful to click the No button and exit a document without saving is if you have made some major unwanted change to a document e.g. a deletion.
Exiting without saving would leave the document as it was the last time it was saved, before you made the unwanted alteration – although you would also also lose any other changes that you had made.

    Now exit the Notepad application again this time taking selecting the **Yes** option on the Dialogue box.

Notes on file names

3.1 ⇨ 95

> In MS-DOS and Windows 3.1 a file name could only consist of up to 8 characters, plus an optional extension of up to three characters, separated from the filename by a full stop or 'dot'. Windows 95 allows file names of up to 255 characters.

Although extensions are still used by Windows 95 to associate a type of file with a particular application the extension is hidden from the user. When a long file name is displayed in an MS-DOS directory display the user only sees the first 8 characters – which may not be unique.

Characters allowed in file names:

The letters A – Z (upper and lower case)

Numbers 0 to 9

A space, a dash (-), a fullstop, a comma, a semicolon, brackets, and underscore (_)

Characters *not* allowed in file names:

Slashes (\ and /), colon and double quotes, also ? * and |

Activity 2 Independent activities

You have now run an application – Notepad – and used it to create some simple text files. Let's experiment with running some other applications. We'll use Wordpad, the word processing application supplied with Windows, to create some more files.

3.1 ⇨ 95

> Wordpad replaces Windows Write as the Windows 95 word processing package.

1. You have already created a number of Notepad documents – see the previous activity; ensure that the diskette storing these files is in A drive.

   Use the **Start** button to open the **Programs** then the **Accessories** menu as before.

   Find the icon labelled **Wordpad** and double click it.

   A blank Wordpad window is displayed, waiting for you to enter some text.

2. Create and save eight dummy files onto A drive in the same way as you did in the Notebook application in the previous activity.

   Use the file names suggested below – not ones of your own.

   Remember to now select the **3 1/2 Floppy (A:)** option to save your work to diskette.

   Make sure that the **Save as type** box reads **Word for Windows 6.** This will save it as a document compatible with Word 6 – Microsoft's word processing package. Various additional formatting characters are added that increase the size of the file.

   SALES – LETTER 1
   SALES – LETTER 2
   SALES – LETTER 3
   SALES – LETTER 4
   ACCOUNTS – LETTER 1
   ACCOUNTS – LETTER 2
   ACCOUNTS – LETTER 3
   ACCOUNTS – LETTER 4

3. When you have created all the above files quit the Windows Wordpad application – this time do so by clicking the Control menu box at the top left corner of the Wordpad Window – see Figure 6.

control-menu icon

Figure 6

   Note. Be careful to identify the correct Control-menu icon, if there are two in view, one for the desktop and one for the Wordpad application, take the one for the Wordpad application.

   Select the **Close** option on the Control-menu.
   The Wordpad application is closed and you are returned to the desktop.

4. **Troubleshooting.** Don't worry if a file name is incorrect – we can put this right later – see Unit 5.

   If the file is the wrong type or stored on the wrong drive it is best to delete it and create it again – see Unit 5.

Activity 3 Other options on the Start menu

As mentioned in Unit 1 the Start menu is the gateway to all essential Windows tasks, ie starting programs, finding files, getting help and exiting Windows. We will briefly review some of the other options that it offers.

1. Click on the **Start** button and select the Documents option. Some of the most recently used files are shown – select one and the file is retrieved. (you may be prompted to insert a disk is the file is on diskette)
   Exit from the file.

2. Select the **Run** option – a dialogue box appears. You can use the Run option to start a program that you can't find using the Programs option (see Activity 2 above) – or sometimes it can be quicker than opening several windows.
   However you will need to know the exact program name, anrd sometimes the drive and folder where it is stored.
   There is a small Help button in the top right hand corner, marked with a question mark – see Figure 7.

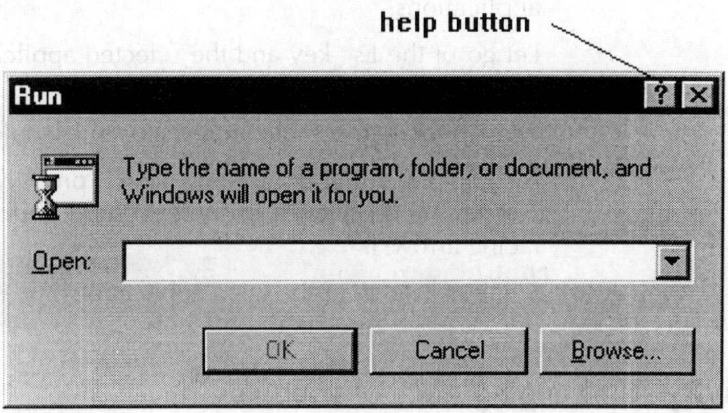

Figure 7

   Click the Help button, then click on any feature of the dialogue box that you want help on.

3. Type **CALC** in the **Open:** box as shown above and click **OK.** The program CALC is run and the calculator appears. Minimise the calculator window – if you are returned to the Run dialogue box then close it.

4. Click the **Start** button and select **Settings** then **Control Panel.**
   A window displays icons which allow you to change various important settings – screen display, keyboard, mouse etc.

   Warning: Casual tinkering with these settings is irresponsible – particularly if you are sharing the PC with others. If in doubt – leave well alone!

5. Double click the **Date/Time** icon – a dialogue box is displayed allowing you to alter the date and time.

6. **Independent activity.** Amend the day, month and year to find what day your next birthday falls. Re-instate the correct date when you have finished and minimise the Date/Time and the Control Panel windows.

7. **Multitasking.** At the moment you are running two applications at once – Calculator and Control panel. They are both minimised and shown as task icons in the Taskbar
   Click both icons and the windows are displayed.

   Open both the **Wordpad** and the **Paint** applications.
   Maximise an application. It should be clear that with multiple windows and tasks displayed in the Taskbar it can be difficult to find the window you want and then bring it to the front in order to work on it.

8. **Showing which application are running.** Press down the **Alt** key. Now press the **Esc** key. The first application that is running is shown. Keep pressing the Esc key an you can cycle through all 4 applications.

   Let go of the Esc key and the selected application is brought to the front.

   The Alt-Esc key combination is a useful supplement to the Taskbar.

   Also try the Alt and Tab keys which produce a similar effect. (the Tab key is on the left of the keyboard and marked with opposite facing arrows).

9. Finally close all of the open applications.

Activity 4 Keeping track of your files

This activity uses the My Computer application to keep track of your files. More advanced features are offered by the Windows Explorer application covered in Unit 4.

3.1 ⇨ 95

> File Manager is replaced by Windows Explorer in Windows 95. However the My Computer application offers a simpler interface for basic operations.
> My Computer allows you view the files that you have. It also allows you to copy, move and delete files, skills that we will be learning in Unit 5.

1. Double click the **My Computer** icon and the window shown in Figure 8 appears.

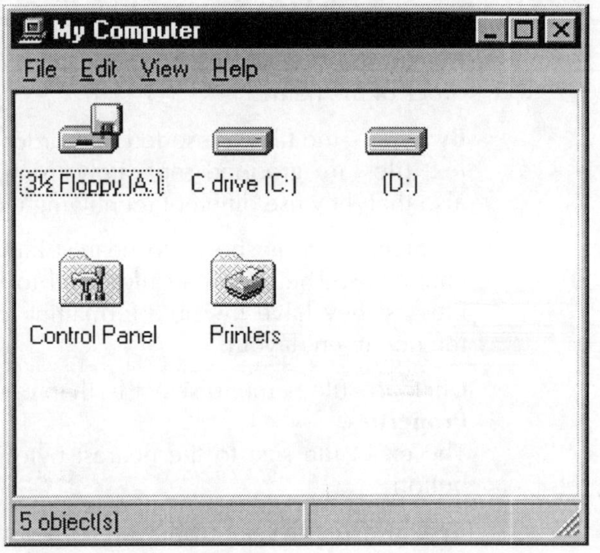

Figure 8

On the desk top are icons representing your computer's resources – printers and disk drives.Your window may be different to this.

2. **Selecting a disk drive.** Insert the diskette containing the files that we have created in the previous activities.

   Look at the disk icons displayed underneath the title bar. The icon for the diskette drive should be shown, marked **3 1/2 Floppy (A:).** Double click this drive icon.
   The files that we have just created should be displayed in a window. If necessary enlarge the window so that all files are visible.
   Check that all 16 files are present – if not return to Activities 1 and 2 and complete them.

   Look at the title of the desktop **3 1/2 Floppy (A:)** This tells you that the disk currently in use is A the floppy or diskette drive.

3. Using the **View** menu at the top of the screen, we can view the files in a variety of ways.

   Open the View menu and try these options in turn:

   Large icons – the file names and icons are enlarged – but fewer will fit in the window

   Small icons – more files can be seen

   List – this is the default display and the best for general use.

   Details – fuller details of the files are displayed – size, type and the date and time of creation/modification. These are discussed more fully in Unit 4.

4. Open the **View** menu and try these **Arrange Icons** options:

By Name is the default option – the files on disk are in alphabetic order of file name.

By Type – the files are sorted into order of their type – the Notepad text files are grouped separately from the Wordpad files. Notice also that they use different identifying icons .

By Size – Size is shown to nearest kilobyte – approximately 1000 characters. The Wordpad files tend to be larger than the Notepad files as they have invisible formatting characters added to control the document layout.

Click any file name to select it, then open the **File** menu and select **Properties.**
The exact file size to the nearest byte is shown. Click the **Cancel** button.

By Date The files are displayed in their order of creation, latest first. Notice that the time of creation is also shown and also determines the order.

5. **Independent activity.**

a. Identify the following files on your diskette:

The largest file.

The file created last – look at the time as well as the date.

Sort the files by name.

b. Click on the column headings – Name, Size etc. The files will be sorted in this order.
Click the same heading again and they are sorted in reverse order. This is a quicker alternative to using the View menu.

Activity 5 Using My Computer to start an application

As you have seen, the My Computer window provides a quick and easy way of finding files on disk; once you have located a file you can open it directly from My Computer.

1. Find the file SALES – MEMO 1 that you created in the Notepad application and double click the icon.
The file will be opened, overlaying the My Computer Window – there was no need to open the Notepad application and then the file, My Computer performs these two operations for you.

2. Close the SALES – MEMO 1 file – open the **File** menu and choose the **Exit** option.

Both the application (Notepad) and the file are closed. You are returned to the My Computer window. As the file was not changed you were not prompted to save it.

3. Now repeat these operations for the file SALES – LETTER 1. The file is a Wordpad document. so this time the Notepad application opens.

   Exit from the document to the My Computer desktop.

4. Exit from **My Computer** too. Don't use the control-menu icon this time; use the alternative method of opening the File menu and selecting **Close.**

Summary of commands

Note

Commands show the object to select first, followed by the command to choose from the menu, e.g. Start Button-Help means click the Start Button and select the Help command. Where a command is available from a particular window this is indicated in brackets.

Alt-Esc/Alt-Tab	Display and change tasks
(My Computer – see Activity 4)	
View	View files on disk in different ways
View-Arrange Icons	View files on disk in different orders
(Notepad)	
Edit-Word Wrap	Move text to new line automatically
(Notepad and Wordpad)	
File-Exit	Quit Application and close file
File-Open	Open existing file
File-Save As	Save new file
File-Save	Save changes to existing file
(Start Button)	
Start-Documents-Run	Run an Application
Start-Programs-Accessories-Notepad	Run Notepad
Start-Programs-Accessories-Wordpad	Run Wordpad
Start-Settings	Change Various System Settings

unit 3

Formatting, copying and printing files

Introduction

In this unit you will learn how to format and copy a diskette, how to print and how to exit Windows.

Skills covered	**Activity**
Application – opening	3
Disk – copying	2
Disk – formatting	1
Document – printing	4
Page – setting up	4.4
Windows – exiting	5

Previous skills required	**covered in unit**
Using the standard Windows components	1

Resources required

The diskette with the practice files created in Unit 2

Activity 1 Formatting a diskette

Introduction

A new diskette it is normally sold unformatted; it cannot be used until it has been formatted. To practice this activity you will need another diskette, preferably new and unused. I am assuming that your PC takes the standard three and a half inch, high density 1.44 Mb diskettes.

Formatting or initialising divides the diskette into electro-magnetic tracks so that information can be stored on it. If you format a used disk then any information already stored on it will erased. It cannot be recovered using Windows, but the MS-DOS Unformat command can restore the information.

Recognising high density disks. All new PC's use the standard three and a half inch, high density 1.44 Mb diskettes. However the older double density 720Kb disks can be read by the newer high density drives.
How many square holes does your disk have? All disks have one – the write protect notch which can be opened to protect the files from being changed. Only high density disks have a second hole – this is your best guide, though some manufacturers stamp 'HD' on their disks.

1. Start Windows if necessary and make sure that My Computer is open.

Insert a new, *unused* diskette in A drive – not the practice diskette.

The files from the previous diskette used may still be displayed.
Double click the A drive icon . My Computer searches the new disk for files.

If you have inserted a new, unformatted disk it will be unreadable and you will receive the message:

'The disk in drive A is not formatted. Do you want to format it now?'

Click the **No** button.

Note: If you inserted a used disk then the files will be displayed, it can be used for this exercise but check that you no longer need any of the files it contains.

Now click the button for the A drive window – *a disk cannot be formatted when its window is open.*

2. Make sure that the A drive icon is still selected.

Open the **File** menu and select **Format** . A dialogue box **Format – 3 1/2 Floppy (A:)** is displayed – see Figure 1.

Click this box and enter a suitable label, eg **backup-files.**

Format Type: If you are using a used disk that has *already* been formatted you can click the Quick (erase) button. A 'blob' appears in it.
If you are using a brand new unformatted disk click the **Full** button.

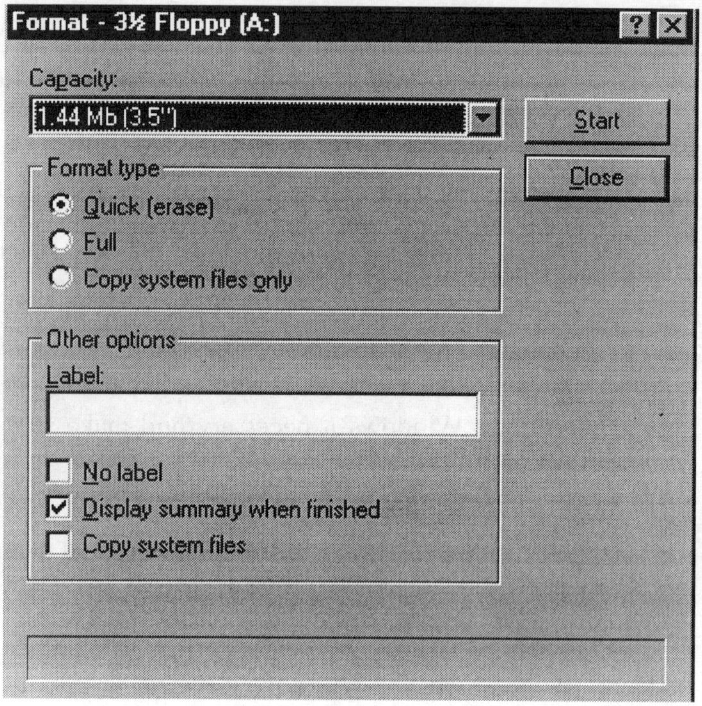

Figure 1

Other options: Make sure that the **Display summary information when finished** option box is checked, ie ticked. A report on the format will be displayed.

System file options: We will be finding out more about system files in a later activity. Leave this option unselected.

The help button: The Format dialogue box offers a special **Help** (?) button at the top right of the window. To find out more about an option click the button then the option.

Finally click the **Start** button.

A formatting bar appears while the formatting takes place – if you are not using Quick Format then this is a fairly slow process.

3. Eventually this is replaced by the following results box – see Figure 2. It reports on the formatting; note that your diskette should now have a storage capacity of 1.44 megabytes – it will hold approximately 1.44 million characters or bytes.

Click the Close button and return to the Format dialogue box.

Unless you wish to format another disk click the **Close** button.

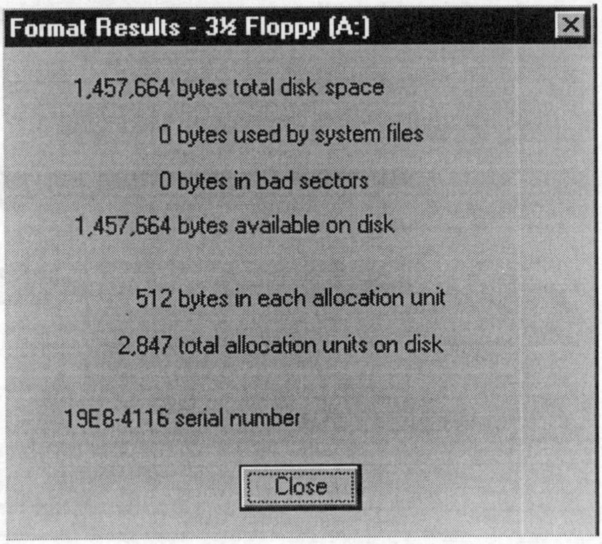

Figure 2

Activity 2 Copying a disk

Introduction

Now that we have formatted a diskette we are going to use it to take a backup copy of the dummy practice files that we have created. Although modern computer media are very reliable there is always the danger that your diskette may be lost, stolen or damaged. It is foolhardy not to back up important data regularly. Diskettes may be cheap to replace, but the data they contain certainly is not!

1. Remove the diskette that you have just formatted from the drive and make sure that it has a label. Write on it the following:

your name and point of contact, e.g. 'J SMITH B Sc 1 Computing'

The disk contents, e.g. 'Backup Windows Dummy Files'.

Make sure that this label is updated when required.

2. Suitably label the original diskette containing the 16 dummy files and insert it in A drive.

If you have *two* diskette drives then put the newly formatted disk in this drive.

Open the **My Computer** window if necessary.

Double click on the icon for the diskette drive.

Check that the 16 dummy files are displayed in the disk window.

Close the disk window and return to the My Computer display.

3. Open the **File** menu and select **Copy Disk.** (If this option is not displayed then click the disk icon to select it, then repeat the command)

4. A dialogue box appears – see Figure 3.

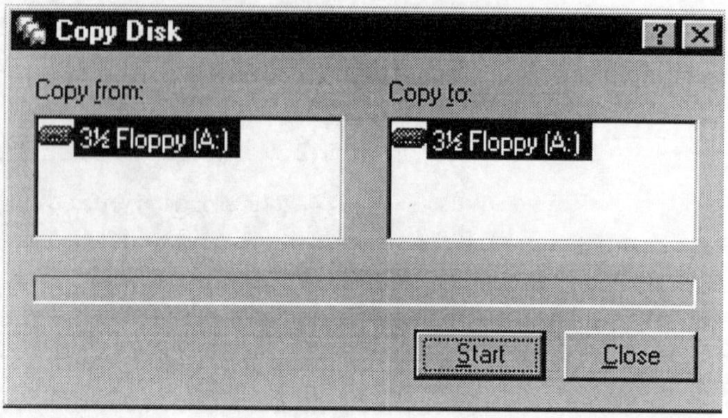

Figure 3

Make sure that **3 1/2 Floppy (A:)** is selected in the **Copy from:** box

If you have *one* diskette drive then also select **3 1/2 Floppy (A:)** in the **Copy to:** box.

If you have *two* diskette drives then select **3 1/2 Floppy (B:)** in the **Copy to:** box.

Click the **Start** button.

A 'Copying Disk' message appears next. The files are being copied from source disk into main memory. This is a fairly slow process which records the progress of the copying.

5. If you are using one disk drive a dialogue box asks you to ' Insert the disk you want to copy to (destination disk)'.
Do this and click the **OK** button.

6. When copying is complete a 'Copying completed successfully' message appears.

Click the **Close** button.

Double click the A drive icon to check that the copied files are copied.

Note: With disks containing more data you may need to swap the source and destination disks over more than once.

7. Remove the backup disk from A drive. As an additional safeguard open the write-protect hole on the disk. This will prevent the files being amended or deleted. You will need to close it again whenever you wish to modify the contents of the disk.

8. Insert the original source diskette in A drive.

Activity 3 Opening a file from within an application

Introduction

We've just seen that the My Computer application allows you to keep track of all the files on your disks. However, if you are already using an application such as Notepad or Wordpad you don't need to exit to My Computer. It's just as easy to find and retrieve a file when you are working in an application.

In this activity we'll be using Wordpad as an example but the steps are essentially the same for all Windows applications – spreadsheets, databases, word processors or whatever.

1. Click the **Start** button and select the **Programs** then the **Accessories** option. Open the **Wordpad** Application.

   A blank Wordpad document appears with the default title 'Document – **Wordpad'**

   You have already created a number of Wordpad documents in the previous unit; ensure that the diskette storing these files is in the diskette drive.

2. Open the **File** menu – notice that the four most recently used Wordpad documents are listed and could be opened.

   Select the **Open** option – the Open dialogue box appears – see Figure 4.

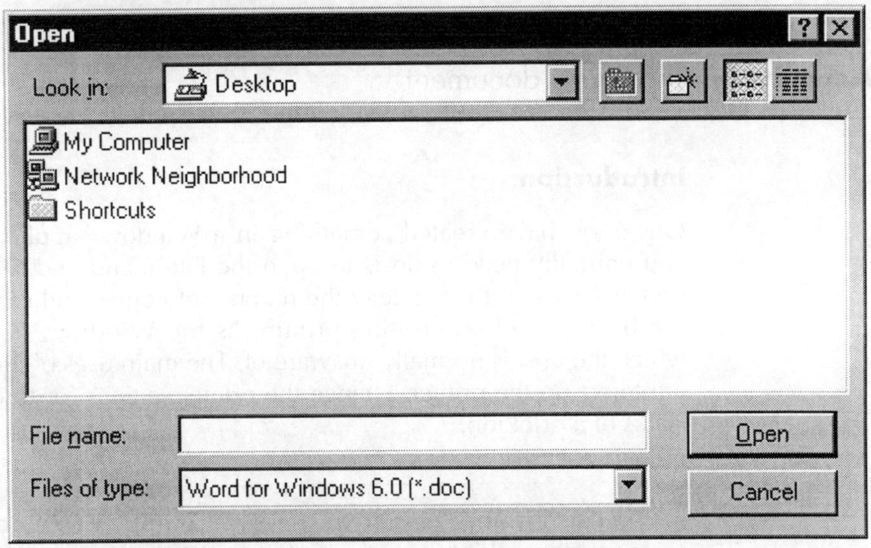

Figure 4

Look at the **Look in** box – is A currently the active drive?

If not click the down arrow button attached to the Look in box. A list box opens.

Click A drive icon to select it.

The File Name box shows 8 Wordpad files, as you are opening a file from the Wordpad application no other type of file on the diskette are listed.

3. Double click on the file name **ACCOUNTS – LETTER 1.**
Windows looks for this file on your diskette (notice that the drive light on the front of the PC lights up)
The Wordpad window appears with the text of the ACCOUNTS – LETTER 1 file.
You now know how to retrieve a file from within an application.

Let's try this once more, this time for the document ACCOUNTS – LETTER 3
Repeat the above steps. The previous document ACCOUNTS – LETTER 1 is closed and the document ACCOUNTS – LETTER 2 replaces it in the Wordpad window.

4. A file can also be retrieved by typing the name in the File Name box.

To retrieve the document SALES – LETTER 1 open the **File** menu and select the **Open** option as before.
Now when the Open dialogue box appears – see Figure 4 above – simply type the filename SALES – LETTER 1 in the File Name box and click **Open.**
This method of typing the file name can be used if you are sure of the file name – it avoids looking through a long list of files.

5. Go on to the next activity now, leaving this document open.

Activity 4 Printing a document

Introduction

Once you have created something in a Windows application all that you normally need to do is to open the File menu and select the Print option. You can then specify the number of copies and other details. In the background controlling printing is the Windows *Printers Folder* which the user is normally unaware of. The main uses of Printers Folder are to set up the printer, change the printer settings, or to check on the status of a print job.

3.1 ➩ 95

The Printers Folder in the My Computer Window replaces Print Manager in Windows 3.1

1. In this activity we will be printing off the Wordpad document SALES – LETTER 1.
If this document is not open then repeat the previous activity

2. **The Printer.** Check that the printer is:

   Switched on.

   Set online – check switch and warning light.

   Connected via cable to your computer.

   Has paper in it.

   Note: If you have no functioning printer you can still carry out the following steps, but an error message will appear if you attempt to print

3. Open the **File** menu in the Wordpad document and select **Print Preview.**

   A window appears showing the layout of your document on the page.

   Zoom in and **Zoom out** will show you this in more or less magnification – try this.

   Click the **Close** button.

4. Open the **File** menu and select **Page Setup.**

   Experimenting with any of the following settings may mean that they are wrongly set for the next document – always check them if your document prints incorrectly.

   A dialogue box appears allowing you to alter paper size and margins.

   Portrait orientation prints down the page in the usual way.

   Landscape orientation prints widthways across the page – useful for wide documents.

   The **Margins** can also be changed.

   Click the **Printer** button – a further window appears showing the type of installed printer. If you are on a network you may have a choice of printers.

   Click the **Cancel** button and return to the Page Setup dialogue box.

   Click **Cancel** again.

5. Open the **File** menu and select **Print.**

   The Print window appears next, showing a dialogue box where you can select the pages and number of copies that you want to print.

   If you are connected to a printer then click the **OK** button.

   A ' Printing' message appears on screen and the document starts to print.

   If you are *not* connected to a printer press the **Cancel** button

6. Finally use the File menu to exit from Wordpad, you are returned to the My Computer desktop.

7. **Other printer settings.** Open the **My Computer** window if necessary.

Double click the **Printers** icon – a window displays the available printer(s).

Select the printer you are going to use.

Open the **File** menu – notice the options to pause and purge (cancel) printing jobs.

Select the **Properties** option from the File menu – a dialogue box appears.

There are 5 tabs (options) along the top – see Figure 5 – many offer settings that that rarely, if ever need adjusting.

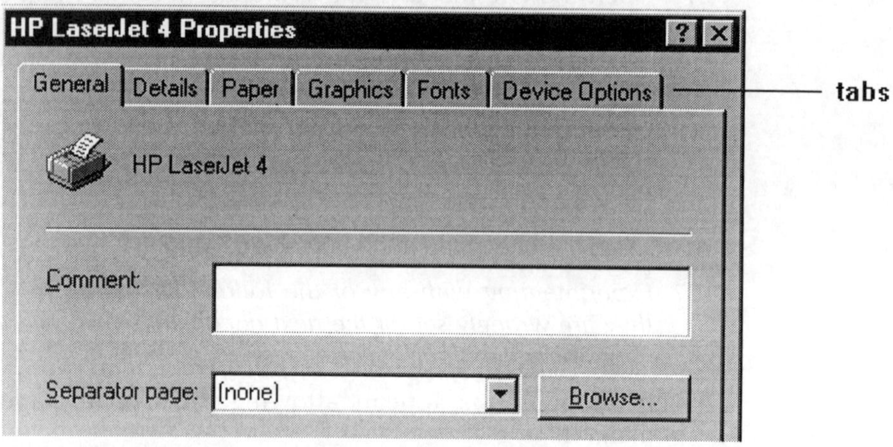

Figure 5

Click the **Paper** tab – this allows you to select different paper sizes.

Click the **Graphics** tab – this allows you to alter the printer resolution for printing graphics.

Click the **Device Options** tab – this allows you select the quality of printed output, eg letter or draft quality, depending on your printer.

Help: Remember that you can get information on a particular feature – click the Help button (top right marked with a '?' sign) then the feature.

8. Close the dialogue box and the **My Computer** window.

Activity 5 Exiting Windows

The Start menu is used to end your Windows session. Do not simply turn off the computer as:

- You may have applications still running and work you have not saved – this will be lost and your files could be damaged.
- If you are on a network you will need to log on and off with a password. This could cause problems next time you log on.

1. Check the taskbar and close down any applications or files that are running – right click on the button then select the **Close** option.

2. Click the **Start** button. A menu appears.

   Select the **Shut down** option – a dialogue box appears offering 4 options or the chance to change your mind – see Figure 6.

   (if you have omitted step 1 you will be reminded to save any changes)

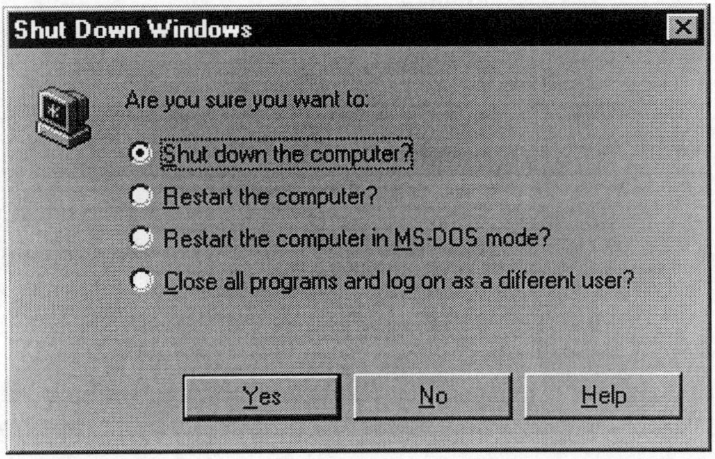

Figure 6

3. Use the Help button to get information about the options – they may vary, depending on whether your PC is connected to a network.

   If you wish to finish then make sure the first option is selected

   If you wish to re-start the computer (perhaps you are experiencing system problems) then select the second option.

   If you are on a network and wish to log-off to allow other users to log on then choose option 4. (if your computer is running MS-DOS then you may be offered this as option 3)

4. Click the **Yes** or **No** button as appropriate.
   If you have been using an application and have omitted to save some work then another dialogue box will prompt you to save it.

5. **Note:** Never turn off the PC without exiting from Window first; even if you have saved your files Windows stores certain information in an area of memory called a cache, eg which windows were opened or closed. This information will be lost if you do not exit properly.

Summary of commands

Note

Commands show the object to select first, followed by the command to choose from the menu, e.g. Start Button-Help means click the Start Button and select the Help command. Where a command is available from a particular window this is indicated in brackets.

(My Computer)	
File-Copy Disk	Copy diskette
File-Format	Format diskette
(From within an Application)	
File-Open	Open an existing file
File-Page Setup	Amend layout of printed page
File-Print	Print file currently open
File-Print Preview	Preview layout of printed page
(Start Button)	
Shut Down	Exit Windows

unit 4

Explorer – viewing and locating files

Introduction

In this unit you will be looking at how files are stored and using the Windows Explorer to locate and sort files on different drives and folders

Skills covered	Activity
Drives – changing	1.6
Explorer – starting	1.2
File Details – viewing	1.10, 2.2
File Extensions – viewing	2.3
File Types – identifying	2.3
Files – displaying	1.9
Files – locating	3
Files – sorting	2.3
Folders – creating	4
Folders – displaying	1.7
Folders – removing	4.4
Folders – renaming	4.3
Path – giving	3
Wild Card Search	3

Previous skills required

Using the standard Windows components – see Unit 1

Resources required

The diskette with the practice files created in Unit 2

3.1 ⇨ 95

> Explorer replaces File Manager. Like File Manager it allows you to display the folders and files on your PC, however unlike File Manager there is no need to open a new window for every drive, you can review the contents of all your drives using one window.
>
> In Windows 95 a directory is now called a folder.

If you are used to File Manager then you may prefer the My Computer to the Explorer display for simple folder structures – see Unit 2. Explorer is easier to use for browsing multiple drives and levels of folder, but My Computer makes it possible to view the contents of two folders simultaneously

What does Explorer do?

Explorer performs the basic 'housekeeping' tasks associated with organising and maintaining your files, you can :

Change from one disk drive to another

Change from one folder to another

Create a structure of folders

View the files that you have in a variety of ways – by size, date, type etc

Copy, rename, move and delete files

Format and copy whole disks.

You'll need to perform all these tasks sooner or later.

Do I need Explorer to perform these tasks?

It is possible to carry out at least some of the above tasks while you are using an application. However there will be situations when you are in Windows and want to review and tidy up your files – located perhaps in several folders or diskettes. In this situation Explorer is the quickest and easiest option to use. Explorer can also be used to start up applications.

Activity 1 Fundamental ideas – files, folders and drives

This activity introduces you to the the various parts of the Explorer window. Along the way it explains the key concepts of file, folder and drive.

1. Insert the diskette containing the practice files that you created in Unit 2 into the diskette drive. We will be using them in the activities that follow.

2. **Starting up Explorer from the Start menu.** Open the **Start** menu and select the **Programs** option and then choose **Windows Explorer** – the Explore Window opens.

   Maximise the window.

   The window shown in Figure 1 appears.

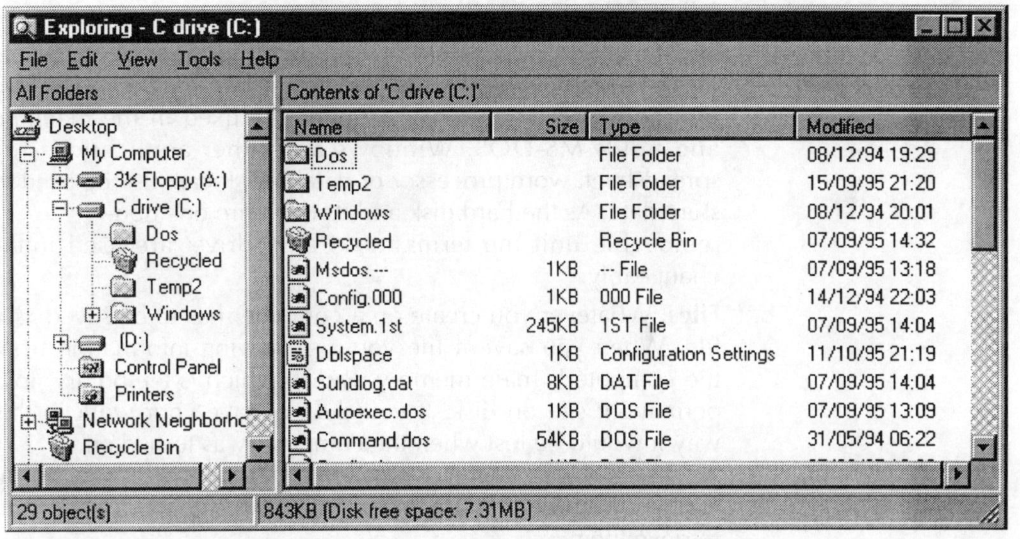

Figure 1

   It contains the now familiar Windows features – title, menu and scroll bars, plus maximise, close and minimise buttons.

   In the window are icons representing files, folders and disk drives. Don't worry if yours differ from mine, we'll be working on ones that are common to all Windows systems.

3. **Troubleshooting.** If the right hand side of your display does not conform to this overall layout check that the **Details** option is selected on the **View** menu.

4. **The Explorer Window.** The Explorer window is split into two halves:

   a. The left side shows the various drive icons – a, b, c etc, plus the various folders they contain.

   b. the right side – at the top is the label and /or letter for the disk or network drive currently being read. If you look at Figure 1 above you will see that the drive currently selected is C. I have labelled it C Drive. Yours may have no label, in which case only the drive letter C: will be shown.

      Underneath are the files in the drive or folder currently selected.

      Drives, folders and files are your three basic units of organisation and we are going to take some time to explore them.

5. Concepts and terminology

a. **Disk drives.** Your computer probably has at least two drives, the diskette drive, known as A drive, and the hard disk, known as C drive. You may well have other drives, e.g. you may be connected to a network or have a CD-ROM drive.

Whenever you refer to a drive you do so using the letter followed by a colon symbol, e.g. a: or c: (upper or lower case)

The diskette drive is used to store data in a portable form (i.e. on diskettes or floppy disks which can be removed) The hard disk and its drive unit are permanently fixed in the machine and holds MS-DOS, Windows and other applications, eg spreadsheet, word processor or database. It can also be used to store data. As the hard disk and its drive are one non-removable unit the terms 'disk' and 'drive' are used interchangeably.

b. **Files.** Whatever you create on a computer has to be saved as a file. When you save a file you are copying information from the computer's main memory (RAM), which is temporary, to a permanent site on disk. If you did not save your work in this way it would be lost when the computer was turned off.
A file on a computer is similar to a paper file in a filing cabinet. Both need a file name in order to file them away and retrieve them.

c. **Rules for file names.** In Windows 95 a file name can consist of up to 255 characters, these can be the letters A to Z (upper or lower case) or numbers 0 to 9.

Certain other keyboard characters can be used, including the dash (-)and the underscore character (_).

The following cannot be used : ? * " < > | \ and /

Although extensions are still used by Windows 95 to associate a type of file with a particular application the extension is hidden from the user. The different types of file are dealt with more fully in Activity 2

d. **Folders.** A diskette can store dozens of files, a hard disk can store hundreds. To make files easier to locate they are grouped into separate folders. Large folders containing usually divided into further subfolders – like drawers in a filing cabinet.. A typical structure is shown in Figure 2.

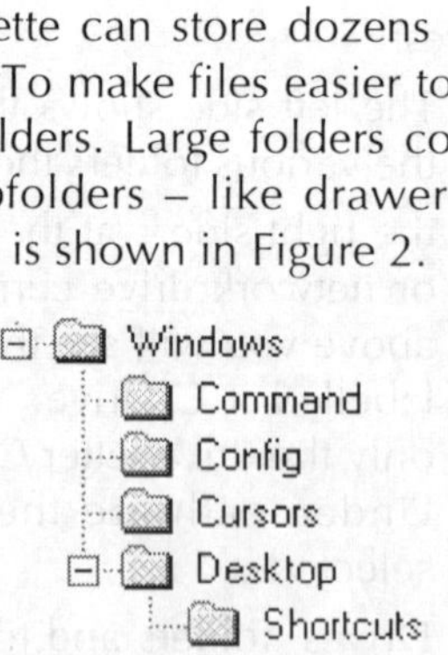

Figure 2

It illustrates the tree structure adopted by Windows. The drive is divided into many folders,each of which in their turn can be divided into further files and subfolders, like branches on a tree.

The Windows folder holds a collection of further subfolders – Command, Config, Cursors and Desktop. Desktop holds a further subfolder called Shortcuts

Let's see how your files and folders are stored. (Remember that they will be different to the ones on my PC)

Note for MS-DOS and Windows 3.1 Users

When a long file name is displayed in an MS-DOS directory display the user only sees the first 8 characters – which may not be unique, so MS-DOS avoids duplicate file names by adding a number to them, eg

Sales.Report.Muir.August 94 is shown as SALESR~1.AUG

Sales.Report.Muir.August 95 is shown as SALESR~2.AUG

You will need to consider this if you create files in in Windows 95 and use them in Windows 3.1 or MS-DOS.

6. **Changing drives.** Look at the drives displayed in the left hand window. The drive icon itself is shown, plus an an open/close button marked with a + sign for closed or a – sign for open. If no drives are shown click the open/close button next to the My Computer icon.

   Click on the icon for **C** drive – it is highlighted indicating that it is now the 'active' drive. Only one drive can be active at one time.

   Click the **A** drive icon. A is now the active drive.
   The title of the window changes to reflect this.

   Now change back to **C** drive.

7. **Displaying folders.** Don't worry about the right hand window yet.

   Go through the list of drives on the left hand side of the window and click the open/close buttons so that they are all closed – showing a + sign.

   Now click the open/close button next to the C drive icon – the list expands showing the folders on this drive – see Figure 3. In the left hand window C remains the selected or active drive.

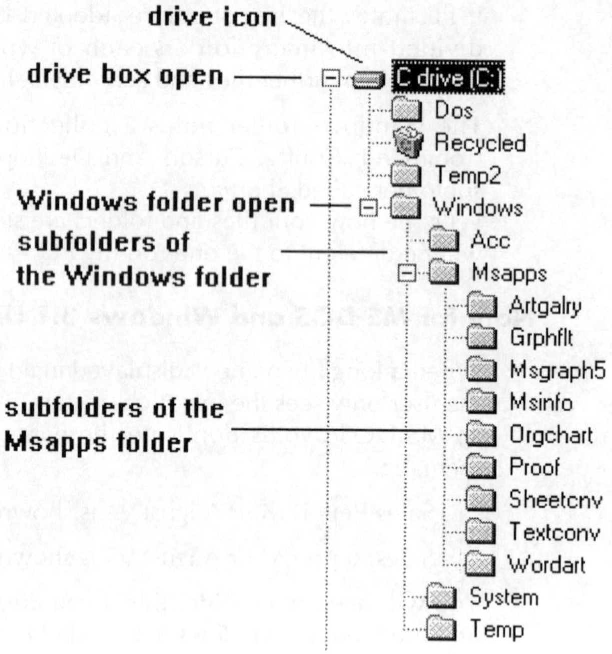

Figure 3

Click again and the C drive open/close button is closed.

Now open the other drives – the list becomes quite long and you may need to use the scroll bar.

8. **Displaying subfolders.** Find the **Windows** folder – it is usually located on C drive. Open the **Windows** folder – it opens to display further subfolders – see Figure 4.

The Windows folder contains all the files necessary to run Windows 95. It is divided into various levels of subfolders as a tree or hierarchy. (a folder containing other subfolders is marked with a + sign)

Some subfolders contain further subfolders – open the System folder and further subfolders are shown. None of these have an open/close button so they contain no further folders, only files. Close the System Folder using the open/close button.

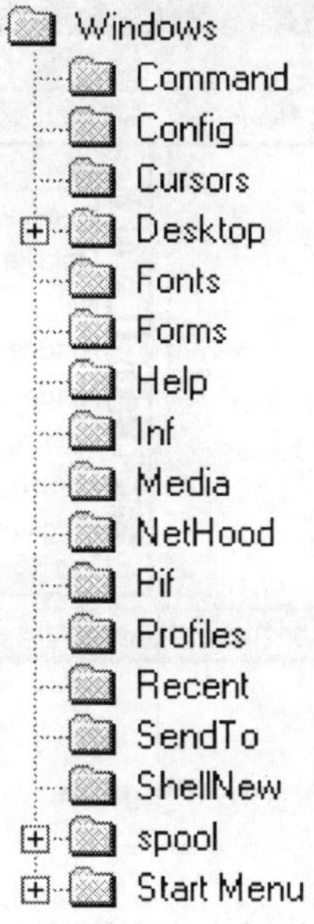

Figure 4

9. **Displaying files.** Whenever you click on the folder or drive icon (as opposed to the open/close button) the right hand window shows you the files and other folders that it contains. Try this as follows:

   Make sure that the drive containing the **Windows** folder is still selected.

   Close the drive using the open/close button – in the right hand window the files and folders on this drive are still shown.

   Open the drive using the open/close button – the right hand display doesn't change.

   Now click the Windows folder to select it – Windows is selected as the 'current' folder and the icon changes to show the folder as open.
   The title bar and the files listed in the right hand window also change.

   Use the scroll bar on the right hand window to review the contents of the Windows folder – some of the files necessary to run Windows are displayed – see Figure 5.
   Scroll through the list. Some of them you may recognise, eg Notepad. You will find that you can display more files at a time if you open the **View** menu and select **List** .

   You can also use the mouse to drag the dividing line between the two halves of the folder screen to the left (marked on Figure 5) – don't overdo this.

   Keep the Windows folder open.

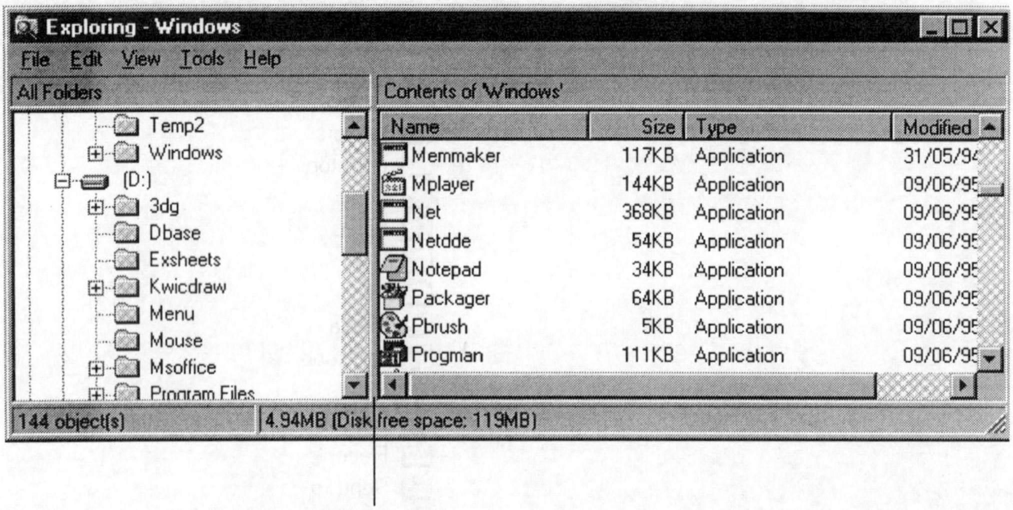

Figure 5

10. **Displaying subfolders – the View menu**. The View menu at the top of the Explorer screen offers various ways of viewing the folders for your disk.

    Open the **View** menu and select these options in turn:

    Large Icons – only useful when viewing a small number of icons.

    Small Icons – displays the maximum number of files/folders.

    List – same as Small Icons except the icons are displayed vertically

    Details – shows details of file size, type and date. The heading over each column can be dragged to narrow or widen it – try this.

    Click the column heading over each column – it sorts the listing on that column – by name, size, type etc.
    Click the heading again and the order is reversed. Notice that folders are not sorted in this way, only files.

11. **Independent activity.** Double click some of the other subfolders in the Windows folder and view their contents using the right hand window.
    Finally use the left hand window to close all the open folders so that only drive icons are shown.

Activity 2 Viewing different file types

In the previous activity we explored the three key file management ideas of,

Drive – your drive is used to either read information from or write information to your disk. Normally the drive is set to either your diskette in A drive or your internal hard disk – usually C drive.

Folder – the disk may be divided into folders, which may divided into further subfolders.

File – Everything stored on disk is saved using a file name. Groups of related files are stored in folders.

In this activity we'll be finding out more about the different type of files.

1. Make sure that the **Explorer** window is open and the contents of the Windows folder still displayed in the right hand window. If necessary enlarge the Explorer window so that a reasonable number of files can be viewed.
2. **File details**. Open the **View** menu and select the **Details** option.

   A display resembling Figure 6 appears.

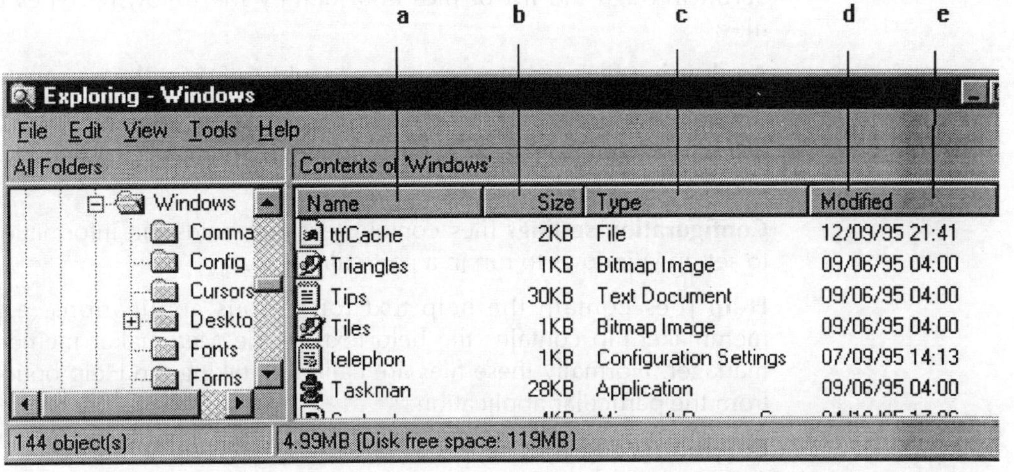

Figure 6

They have been labelled a – e for reference

a. The file **name.** Notice that the icon design helps to indicate the type of file,

b. The file **size** in kilobytes. One byte holds the equivalent of a character, eg a keyboard character such as), 0 or c, as well as special characters normally invisible to the user. In an executable program file a byte holds one machine instruction. A kilobyte or 1K is roughly 1,000 bytes (actually 1024 bytes), a megabyte or Mb equals about a million bytes.

   Click (not double click) a few file names – along the bottom of the window is shown the exact size of the file currently selected.

   Click elsewhere on the window to deselect the file.

   When no file is selected then the total size of the current disk, the total number of files in the current folder and the free disk space is shown.

c. The file **type** – see below.

d and e. The **date** and **time** that the file was created or last modified. Many files will share the same date and time – when they were first installed on disk.

3.1 ⇨ 95

> If you wish to see the file extensions open the **View** menu and select **Options.** Then click the **Hide MS-DOS file extensions** box to deselect it and click **OK.**

3. Click on the **Type** heading to sort the files into type.

Folders are always listed first in alphabetical order, then a number of different file types are listed – this is a good time to review them. Scroll through the list of files and identify the following types of files:

Application files are program files – double clicking them executes or runs them. Normally it is easier to run them from the Start menu.

Bitmap Image files are files containing graphic images, eg windows patterns and backgrounds.

Configuration settings files contain text that holds the information to set up Windows to run in a particular way.

Help files contain the help text for various applications, e.g. memmaker.hlp contains the help text for the Memmaker memory manager. Normally these files are called by taking the Help option from the particular application.

Program group files represent the various group windows; e.g. Accessor represents the accessories group window.

Text document files contain only the basic keyboard characters a to z and 0 to 9, plus punctuation marks and other typable keyboard characters. They are also referred to as ASCII files (American Standard Code for Information Interchange), indicating that they contain only the standard characters. We have used the Notepad application in previous activities to produce these text files.
In the Windows Folder they contain information about Windows which can be called up, sometimes from within an application, eg Tips, Readme.

4. **Independent activity – Opening files from Explorer**.You can use Explorer to open any document or run a program application.

Make sure that the Windows folder and sort the files into Name order.
Double click the following icons – *you will need to close the document or application before opening the next one.*

Accessor – the Accessories group window opens.

Bubbles – the bubbles design is shown in the Paint application window

Calc – the calculator application is run.

Printers – a Notepad document is displayed

Open the **Fonts** subfolder and double click **Arial** – the font is displayed.

Activity 3 Searching for a file or folder

With so many files and folders it can be difficult to find the one you want. Explorer provides a search facility which helps you locate files or folders anywhere on your PC, providing you can remember at least part of the name. If you are not familiar with the MS-DOS syntax for referring to drives, folders and files then read this next part.
However in practice in Windows 95 the wild card characters are often unnecessary.

a. **The Path**. It is important to give the exact location or *path* where the file is stored, ie which *drive* and *folder* (if any)
The drive is always referred to by its drive letter followed by a colon, eg A: and B: are diskette drives, C: and D: hard disks.
The folder and/or file names follow the drive letter, separated by a backslash (\ )
eg: If the file JIM.MEMO 1 is on a diskette in A drive you must give its full path:

A:\JIM.MEMO 1

If the file SALES_FIGURES_AUGUST is in the SALES folder on C drive then the full path is

C:\SALES\SALES_FIGURES_AUGUST

Note that there are no spaces between the colon, slash, drive, folder and file names.

b. **Wild card searching.** If you cannot recall the exact file name or wish to find files with similar names then you will need to use the 'wild card' * and ? characters:

The * or 'star' can stand for any number of characters, eg:

*.AUGUST means any file name ending in the letters .AUGUST

LET*.* means a file name starting with the the three characters LET and ending in anything.

. signifies all files (any name, any extension)

The ? symbol substitutes for individual characters; suppose that you want to find all file names containing the three characters ACC in positions 5 to 7 of the file name, eg MEM-ACCOUNTS 1 or LET-ACCOUNTS 2

So the file name ????ACC* means 'starting with any four characters, then the characters ACC, then any other characters at the end (*)'

1. Make sure that the **Explorer** window is open. If necessary enlarge the Explorer window so that a reasonable number of files can be viewed.
2. Insert the diskette containing the practice files that you created in Unit 2.
3. Select the icon for the diskette drive – the 16 practice files are displayed.
4. Open the **Tools** menu and select the **Find** then the **Files or folders** option. The Find window is displayed, maximise it.
5. Check that the **Look in:** box is set to read the diskette drive; if not click the down arrow key and select it from the list.
6. Make sure that the **Named:** box is blank and click the **Find now** button.
   All 16 files are displayed.
7. Now enter **memo** in the **Named:** box and click the **Find Now** button.
   The 8 files containing the letters 'memo' in their name are listed.
8. Now click the **Named:** box to highlight the search term **memo.** Amend it to **sales** and click the **Find Now** button – 8 files are listed containing these letters.
9. Now try out the following search terms and note the results:

   cc

   1

   let
10. **Reviewing the files that you find.** Once you've located a group of files you may want to quickly review their contents. Quick View allows you to do this without waiting for a large application such as a word processor to load.
    Right click one of the Wordpad files that you created and select **Quick View.**
    The document opens. Try this with several documents, it's quicker than opening them in Wordpad.

    Note: If this option is not available then Quick View has not been installed.
11. **Independent activities**.
    a. **Searching by date.** Use the Look in: box to change to the drive where the Windows folder is located. (see previous activity)

       Click the **Date Modified** tab at the top of the **Find** window.

       Find all files modified in the last 2 months.

    b. **Searching by file type.** Click the **Advanced** tab at the top of the **Find** window.

       Click the down arrow on the **Of type:** box.

       Find all text document files.

As you have seen, the Find command provides a quick and easy way of finding files on disk; once you have located a file you can then open it directly from the Find dialogue box or from Explorer. You can often use the Find command to list certain files as a preliminary to moving, copying or deleting them, activities that we will be practising in future activities.

Activity 4 Making and renaming folders

In previous units we created 16 dummy files, eight using the Notepad text editor application and eight using the Wordpad word processor application.

These are:

SALES – MEMO 1
SALES – MEMO 2
SALES – MEMO 3
SALES – MEMO 4
SALES – LETTER 1
SALES – LETTER 2
SALES – LETTER 3
SALES – LETTER 4
ACCOUNTS – MEMO 1
ACCOUNTS – MEMO 2
ACCOUNTS – MEMO 3
ACCOUNTS – MEMO 4
ACCOUNTS – LETTER 1
ACCOUNTS – LETTER 2
ACCOUNTS – LETTER 3
ACCOUNTS – LETTER 4

We are going to organise these files into folders and subfolders; all the files concerned with Sales Department will be placed in a folder SALES and those concerned with the Accounts Department in a folder ACCOUNTS. The folder tree will look like Figure 7:

Figure 7

Note on folder names. Folder Names follow the same conventions as file names – See Activity 1.

1. Make sure that the diskette containing the above files is inserted in the diskette drive.

   Open Explorer and ensure that the diskette drive is selected.

   Click the drive icon to display the files. If the files are not displayed, check that the correct diskette is in the drive and that no Find conditions are still in force from the previous activity.

2. **Creating a new folder.** Open the **File** menu and select **New** then the **Folder** option.
   The new folder appears in the right hand window labelled 'New Folder' – see Figure 8.

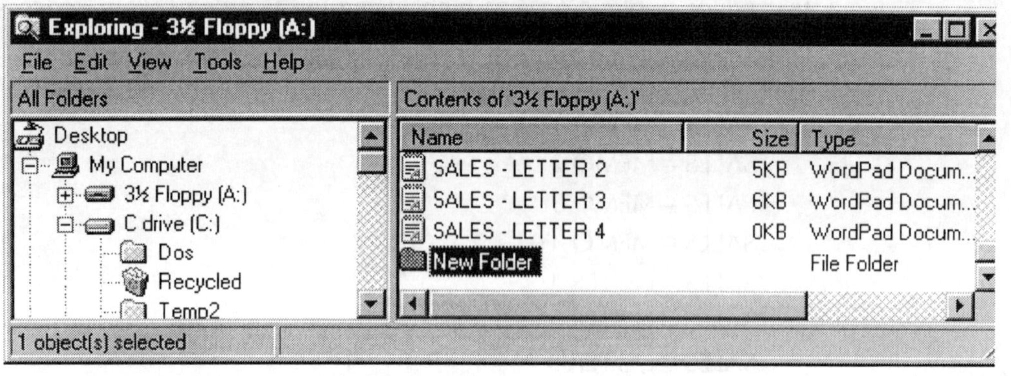

Figure 8

3. **Renaming folders.** Make sure that the new folder is selected.

   Open the **File** menu and select **Rename.**

   Type the name **Sales Folder** and the folder is re-named

   Click elsewhere on the window to deselect the folder.

4. **Removing folders.** Click the Sales Folder once to select it.

   Open the **File** menu and select **Delete.** A dialogue box appears asking you to confirm the deletion.

   Click **Yes.**

   The folder is deleted.

5. Make sure that the diskette drive is still selected.

   Re-create the Sales Folder and a second called Accounts Folder.

   The window should now resemble Figure 9.

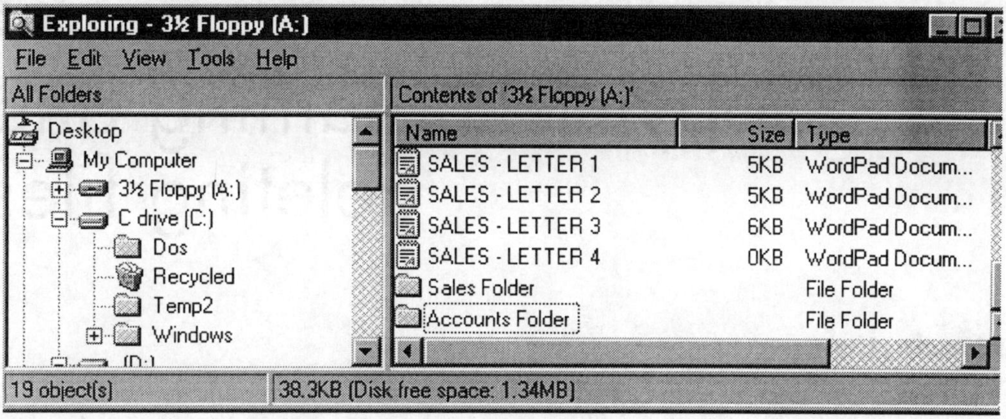

Figure 9

6. Double click each new subfolder in turn – no files or folders are displayed on the right hand side of the screen – as yet there are no files in these subfolders.

Select the diskette drive icon again.

Summary of menu commands

Notes

Menu commands show the menu name first, followed by the command to choose from the menu, e.g. Edit-Clear means open the Edit menu and select the Clear command. Where a command is available from a particular window this is indicated in brackets.

Start-Programs-Windows Explorer	Start Windows Explorer
(Windows Explorer)	
File-Delete	Delete file or folder
File-Rename	Rename folder or file
File-New-Folder	Create new folder
Tools-Find-Files or Folders	Search for named file or folder
View-Details	View all details of files
View-Options	Show/Hide various files/file details
View-Large Icons	View files as large icons
View-Small Icons	View files as small icons

unit 5

Copying, renaming and deleting files

Introduction

In this unit you will be learning how to move and copy files between different folders and disk drives. You will be renaming files and finding out how to delete files and how to recover them from the Recycle Bin.

Skills covered	**Activity**
Files – copying and moving between diskettes	5
Files – copying and moving using menu	4
Files – copying and moving using mouse	1, 2
Files – deleting	7
Files – recovering deleted	8
Files – renaming	6
Folders – deleting	9
Folders – displaying multiple	3
Recycle Bin – using	8

Previous skills required	**covered in unit**
Using the standard Windows components	1

Resources required

The diskette with the practice files created in Unit 2, plus a further blank diskette

Activity 1 Moving and copying individual files

Copying and moving files are essential procedures, typical situations are:

a. Making a copy of a diskette – you have already done this in Unit 3, Activity 2.

b. Copying files from one folder to another.

c. Copying files from hard disk to diskette, eg to create backups, or to work on another PC.

d. Copying files from diskette to hard disk, eg installing a new application.

Because of the threat of viruses most colleges do not allow activity d and/or prevent it by technical means. In this activity we will copy and move files from the main folder into the two new subfolders – Sales and Accounts that we have created in Unit 4. *Moving* a file does just that – removes it to a new location, *copying* a file keeps the original where it is and places the copy in the new location. We will practice both operations.

You can either use the mouse to 'drag and drop' the file in its new location or use the Cut and Paste commands.

1. **Copying files.** Make sure that the diskette containing the practice files is inserted in the diskette drive.

   Open Explorer and ensure that the diskette drive is selected (click once on the icon for the drive, top left of the window). The Folder window should resemble Figure 1.

   If necessary maximise the window so that all files and folders can be seen.

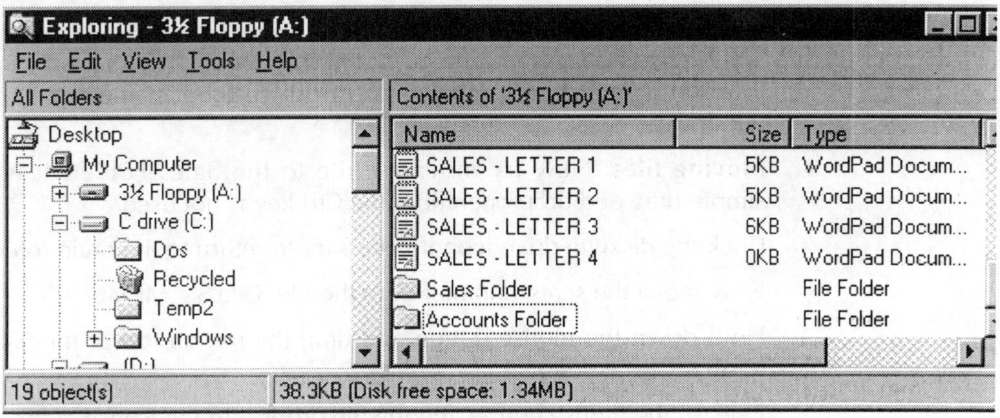

Figure 1

2. Hold down the **Ctrl** key on the keyboard.

   Move the cursor onto the file SALES – MEMO 4.

   Hold down the mouse button and drag the file on top of the icon for the Sales Folder – see Figure 2:

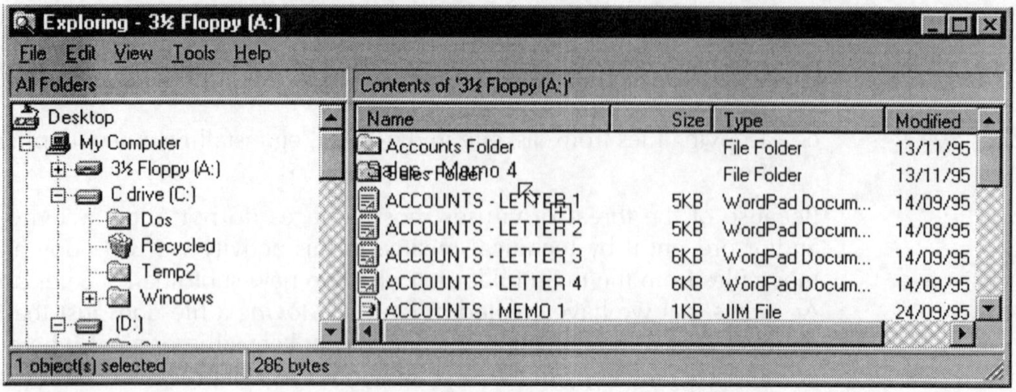

Figure 2

The cursor changes to a file icon with a plus sign – this indicates that the file is being copied rather than moved.

Release the mouse button *then* the Ctrl key. The file drops into the Sales Folder.

A confirmation message appears; this should confirm the file name, the copying operation, and the destination – the Sales Folder.

3. Click the icon for the Sales Folder to check that the the file has actually been copied. Click the icon for the diskette drive (in the left hand window) to check that the original is still there.

Troubleshooting: if you released the Ctrl key too soon then the file will be moved rather than copied. In this case click the Sales Folder to open it and drag the file onto the drive icon in the *left* hand window.

4. **Moving files.** Now try *moving* a file to the Sales Folder. It is a simple drag and drop operation; the Ctrl key is not used.

Click the diskette drive icon if necessary to return to the main folder

Now move the screen pointer onto the file SALES – MEMO 3.

Hold down the mouse button and drag the file on top of the icon for the Sales Folder.

Release the mouse button and the file drops into the Sales Folder.

A confirmation message appears; this should confirm the file name, the move operation, and the destination folder – Sales.

Check that the original is no longer there, then open the Sales Folder to check that the the file has actually been moved to this new location.

There should now be two files in the Sales folder. SALES – MEMO 3 and SALES – MEMO 4. Make sure that your window resembles Figure 3.

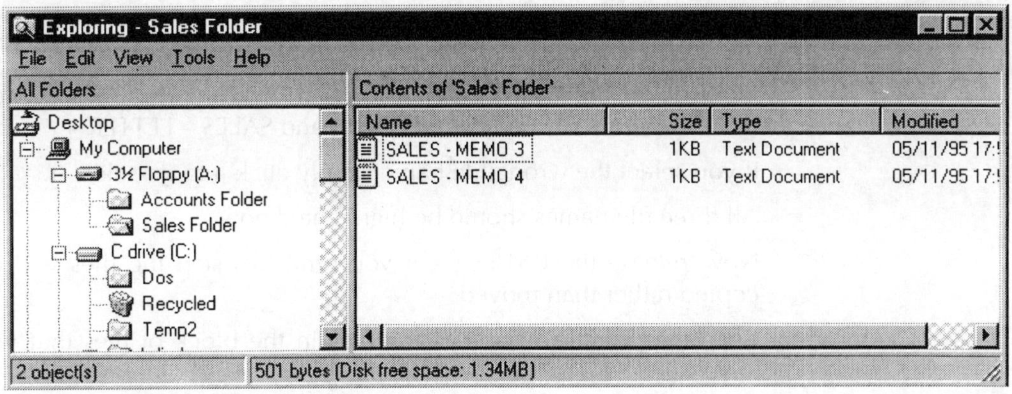

Figure 3

Activity 2 Moving and copying groups of files – Mouse method

1. Now we will copy and move several files at once.

If necessary make sure that the diskette containing the practice files is inserted in A drive, open Explorer and check that the diskette drive window is selected, not a subfolder.

Maximise the window.

2. **Copying groups of files.** First we will copy some of the file names starting with the characters Sales from the main folder to the Sales Folder.

Hold down the Ctrl key and click the following three file names: SALES – LETTER 1, SALES – LETTER 2 and SALES – LETTER 3.

If you select the wrong file name simply click it to de-select it.

All three file names should now be highlighted.

Next, *keeping the Ctrl key pressed down,* keep the pointer on the block of files that you have selected and drag these files onto the Sales Folder icon and release the mouse button *then* the Ctrl key.

A confirmation message appears; this should confirm the copying operation and the destination – the SALES folder.

3. Click the Sales Folder icon to check that the the three files have actually been copied and return to the drive window to check that the originals are still there.

Click on the window to remove the highlight from the copied files

Troubleshooting: If the originals are missing from the root folder then you have moved the files rather than copied them; a common reason is releasing the Ctrl button *before* releasing the mouse button. If this has happened then copy the files back from the SALES to the drive window using the dragging procedure described in section 2.

4. **Moving groups of files.** We will move some more files starting with the characters Sales from the main folder to the Sales Folder.

   Hold down the Ctrl key and click the following three file names: SALES – MEMO 1, SALES – MEMO 2 and SALES – LETTER 4.

   If you select the wrong file name simply click it to de-select it.

   All three file names should be highlighted now.

   Now *release* the Ctrl key – if you omit this step the files will be copied rather than moved.

   Keep the pointer on one of the files in the block of files that you have selected and drag these files onto the Sales Folder icon.

   Release the mouse button.

   A confirmation message appears; this should confirm the move operation and the destination – the Sales Folder.

5. Click the Sales Folder icon to check that the the three files are now in this folder and the drive window to check that they have been moved.

   All 8 files with SALES in their file names should now be in the Sales Folder – see Figure 4; they have been moved or copied there from the drive window. Check this and move or copy them if they are not there.

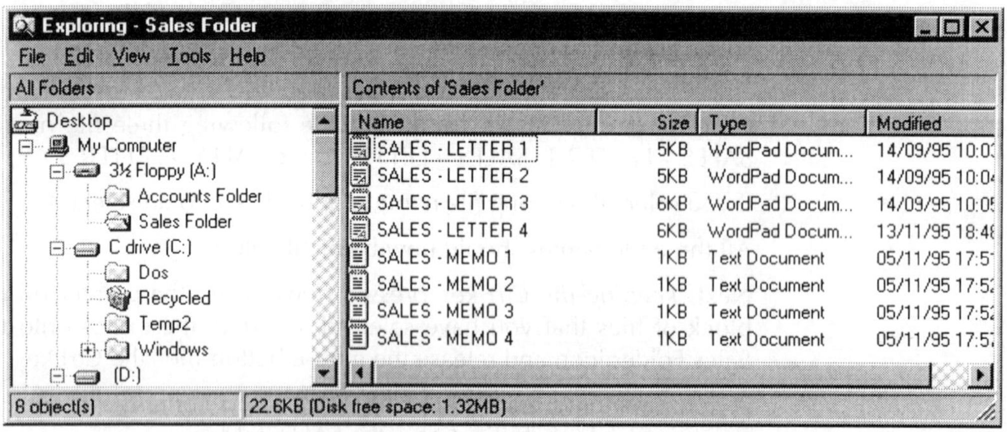

Figure 4

   Troubleshooting. Look in the Accounts Folder; it should be empty; if it contains files with Sales in their file names then move them into the SALES subfolder.

6. Close the Explorer Window.

Activity 3 Displaying two folders

In this activity you will learn how to open more than one folder window at the same time using the My Computer application. This is useful if you want to check and compare the contents of two folders 'side by side' before moving or copying.

1. If necessary make sure that the diskette containing the practice files is inserted in A drive, open **My Computer** and double click on the diskette drive icon. The diskette window opens – a similar display to Explorer, except that the left-hand drives window is not shown.

2. Open the **View** menu and select **Options** – a dialogue box opens.

Make sure that the first option – **Browse Folders using a separate window for each folder** is selected and click **OK.**

3. Double click the icon for the **Sales** Folder – it opens displaying the files.

Now click the icon for the **Accounts** Folder – it should open too.

Check the task bar – four tasks should be running – see Figure 5.

Figure 5

If one of the folders is not visible click the appropriate button in the taskbar.

The two windows can be made smaller if necessary so that all files are still visible – see Figure 6

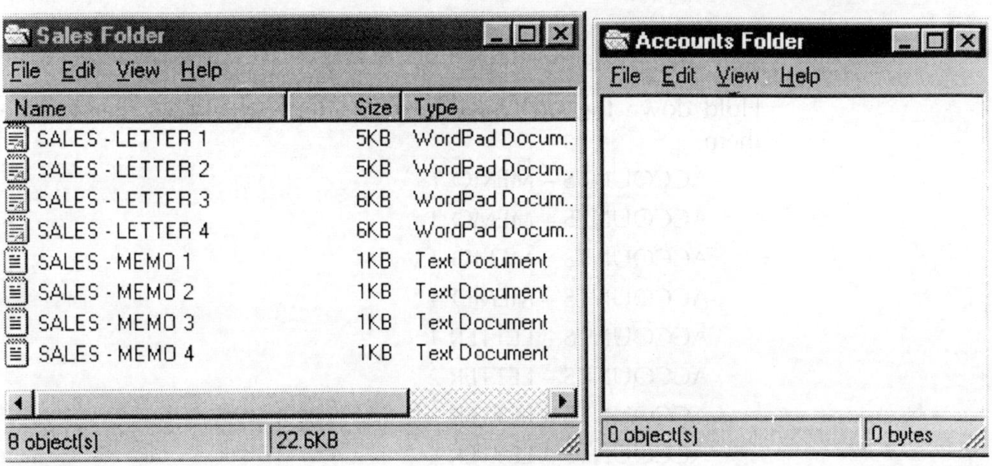

Figure 6

This two windows display allows you compare their contents and to copy or move files.

3.1 ⇨ 95

> If you are used to File Manager then you may prefer the My Computer to the Explorer display for simple folder structures. The drive tree diagram makes Explorer easier to use for browsing multiple drives and levels of folder, but My Computer makes it possible to view the contents of two folders simultaneously.

4. Hold down the Ctrl key and drag the file **Sales – Letter 1** from the Sales to the Accounts folder. Check that the original is still in the Sales Folder.
5. Close all the My Computer windows.

Activity 4 Copying and moving groups of files – Menu method

To copy and move files successfully using drag and drop techniques requires both the source files and the destination folder or drive to be visible in the window. If there is a long list of files or folders it may be difficult to locate the destination that you want to copy to. In this case you may find it easier to use the Move or Copy commands on the Edit menu.

1. **Copying groups of files.** If necessary make sure that the diskette containing the practice files is inserted in the diskette drive, open Explorer and check that the diskette drive window is selected, not a subfolder.

   Maximise the window.

2. We are going to copy all the files concerned with accounts into the Accounts Folder.

   Hold down the **Ctrl** Key and click the following 8 files to select them.

   ACCOUNTS – MEMO 1
   ACCOUNTS – MEMO 2
   ACCOUNTS – MEMO 3
   ACCOUNTS – MEMO 4
   ACCOUNTS – LETTER 1
   ACCOUNTS – LETTER 2
   ACCOUNTS – LETTER 3
   ACCOUNTS – LETTER 4

3. Open the **Edit** menu and select **Copy**

   Double click the destination folder **Accounts Folder** to open it.

Open the **Edit** menu again and select **Paste.** A dialogue box should confirm that copying is taking place.

The eight files have been copied – see Figure 7.

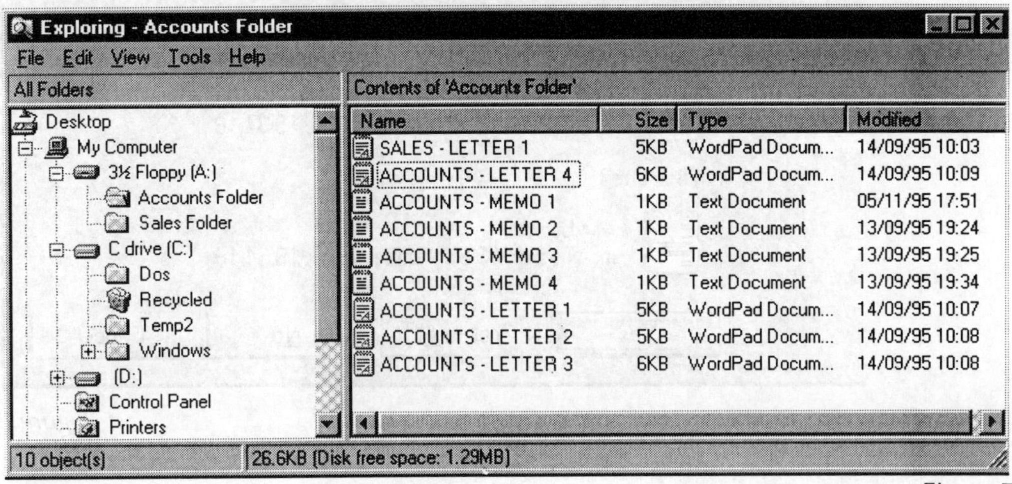

Figure 7

4. **Copying the same file more than once.** You may wonder what would happen if we copied the same files again; would we create files with identical names in the same folder? The answer is no! Windows only permits identical file names in different folders. (we have this situation with the files that we just copied, the original eight files are still in the drive window and the copies in the Accounts Folder)

   If you copy the same files twice the originals are overwritten by the copies. This is useful when you want to replace an original with a new version of a file – there is no need to delete the original, just copy over it. However if you have created two completely different files with the same name you would need to rename one of them.

   To make this point repeat the copy command above. This time you are warned that the original files in the Accounts folder will be overwritten – see Figure 8.

   You can tell by the size and creation date that the two files are identical, click **Yes.**

   The next file to be copied is confirmed; if you are satisfied click Yes again. This process will continue until all the original copies are replaced.

   Click **No** if for any reason you do not want the original overwritten.

   Click **'Yes to All'** if you want all the originals overwritten without further confirmation messages.

5. **Moving files using the Edit-Cut command.** We will not practise this command specifically as it is exactly the same principle as the Copy command that we have just carried out.

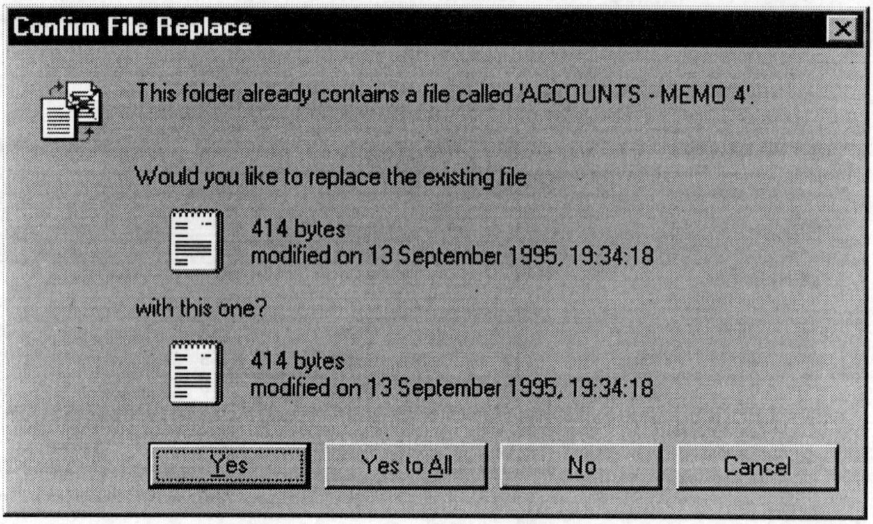

Figure 8

Activity 5 Copying files between diskettes

If you only have one diskette drive (the usual situation) then you may wonder how you can copy files from one diskette to another. An easy way is to use the main desktop as a temporary holding area while you swap over the diskettes. We will try this with our two practice disks.

1. Insert practice disk b that contains the practice files

   Open Explorer if necessary and check that the diskette drive window is selected, not a subfolder.

   Adjust the size of the window so that the main desktop is in view.

2. Select one of the practice files in the right hand window and use the mouse to drag it onto the desktop – see Figure 9.

3. Now eject the diskette and insert practice disk a.

   Open the **View** menu and select **Refresh** to display the files and folders on this diskette.

4. Drag the file from the desktop to the right hand window (not into one of the folders)
   It is copied to the second diskette. If you get a 'Confirm File Replace' message – see figure 8 above – then click the **Yes** button.

5. Finally delete the file from the desktop by dragging it into the Recycle Bin.

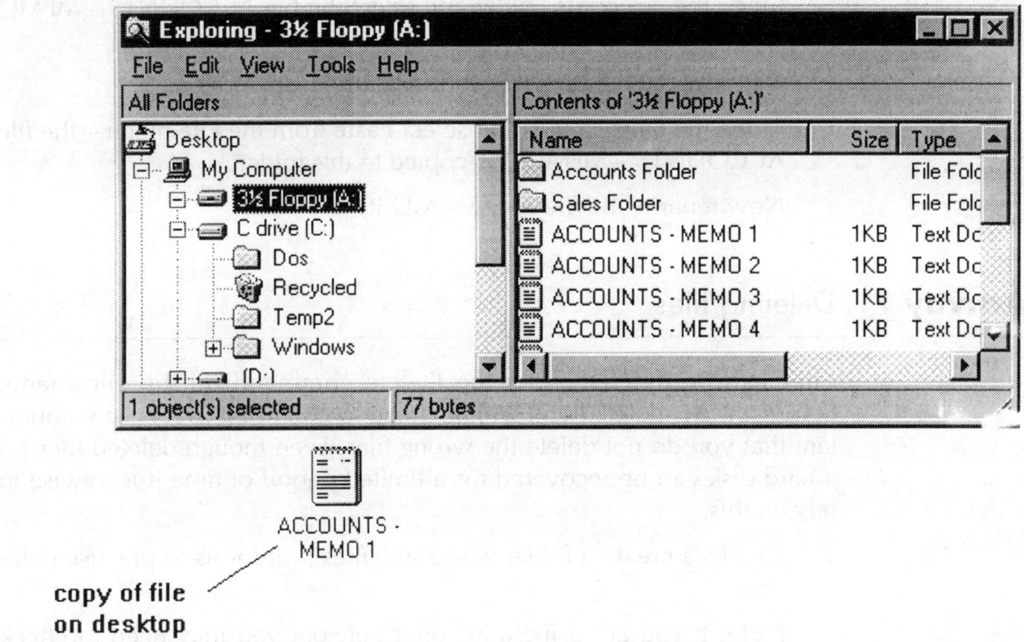

Figure 9

Activity 6 Renaming files

Often we need to need to change the name of a file, perhaps because it is incorrect, or to distinguish it from an earlier or later version. We can simply rename the existing file or make a copy of it under another name. We will try both of these.

1. **Renaming a file without copying.** If necessary make sure that practice diskette a is inserted in the diskette drive, start Explorer and open the Sales Folder and select the file SALES – LETTER 1 (click it once)

   We will give it the extension .JM to identify the author, ie SALES – LETTER 1.JM

2. Open the **File** menu and select the **Rename** option – the file name can now be altered.

   Move the screen pointer to the end of the file name and click once – a text insertion cursor is placed there.

   Add the extension **.JM** then click elsewhere on the window to deselect it.

3. **Copying and re-naming.**

   Let's copy the file ACCOUNTS – MEMO 4 from the Accounts to the Sales Folder, re-naming it SALES – MEMO 5

Open the **Accounts** Folder and select the file ACCOUNTS – MEMO 4.

Next open the **Edit** menu and select the **Copy** option.

Open the **Sales** Folder and select **Paste** from the **File** menu – the file ACCOUNTS – MEMO 4 is copied to this folder.

Now rename the file SALES – MEMO 5

Activity 7 Deleting files

Files can be deleted using the Delete command on the File menu. Before a file is deleted you will be asked to confirm it as it is very important that you do not delete the wrong files. Even though deleted files on a hard disk can be recovered for a limited period of time it is unwise to rely on this.

1. First let's create a folder with some files in it for us to practise deletion.

   Note: If you are using a PC on a network you may need to check whether you can create a folder on a hard drive.

   Make sure that one of the diskettes containing the practice files is inserted in the diskette drive, open Explorer and make sure that the main hard drive window (eg C: or D:)is selected, not a subfolder. The right hand window should read, eg, 'Contents of '(D:)''

   Maximise the window.

2. First let's create a folder with some files in it for us to practise deletion. It will be named Test.

   Open the **File** menu and select **New** then **Folder.**
   The new folder is listed in the window.

   Amend the name to **Test** using the **File – Rename** option.

3. Now, using the operations that you learnt in Activity 4, copy all the files from the **Sales** Folder on the practice diskette to the **Test** subfolder on the hard drive.

   (Hint: you can use the Edit – Select All command to select all the files in the folder before copying them)

4. Open the Test subfolder; check that you have the files listed in Figure 10. If not you will need to copy them over again.

5. **Deleting individual files.** Select the file SALES – LETTER 2.

   Open the **File** menu and select **Delete.**

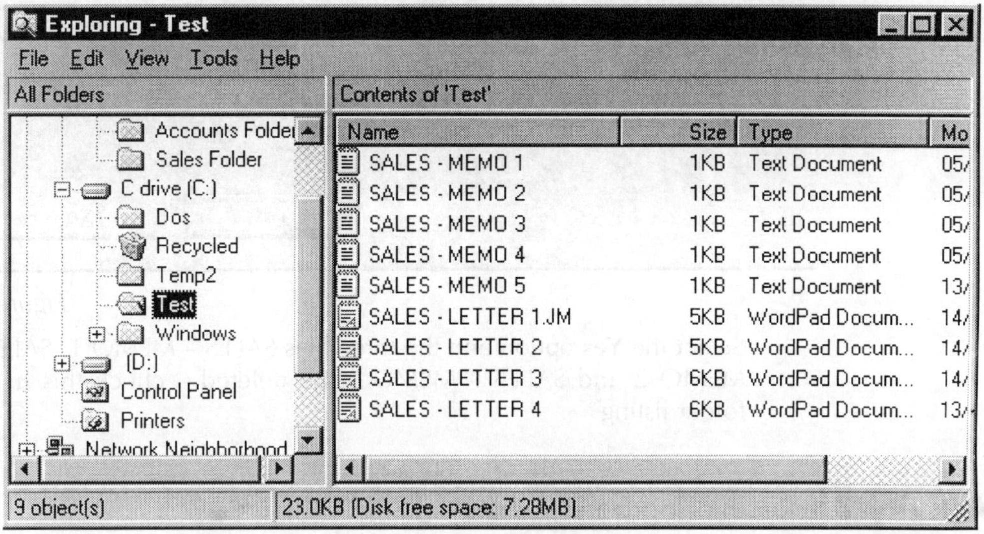

Figure 10

The following dialogue box appears, confirming the file that you have specified for deletion.

You are offered the chance to change your mind. Check you have chosen the correct file.

Click the **Yes** button and the file SALES – LETTER 2 is deleted – check this in the file listing.

6. **Deleting several files.** Hold down the **Ctrl** key and select files SALES – MEMO 1, SALES – MEMO 2, and SALES – MEMO 3.

   Open the **File** menu and select **Delete.**

   A dialogue box appears, notice that the 3 file names are not specified so you must be absolutely sure you have selected the right files – see Figure 11.

Figure 11

Select the **Yes** option and the three files SALES – MEMO 1, SALES – MEMO 2 and SALES – MEMO 3 are deleted – check this in the folder listing.

Activity 8 Recovering deleted files

In Windows 95 deleted files are stored in the Recycle Bin and can be recovered. However space is limited – normally to about 10% of the total space on the drive – and the oldest files are permanently deleted when the recycle bin is full. This means that if you leave deleted files for too long you may not be able to recover them.

It is good practice to open the recycle bin periodically and clear out files you are certain you no longer need – it also saves on disk space.

1. Minimise the Explorer window if necessary. Find the Recycle Bin icon on the main desktop and double click to open it. The window is similar to the Explorer display and shows the files deleted in the last activity – see Figure 12.

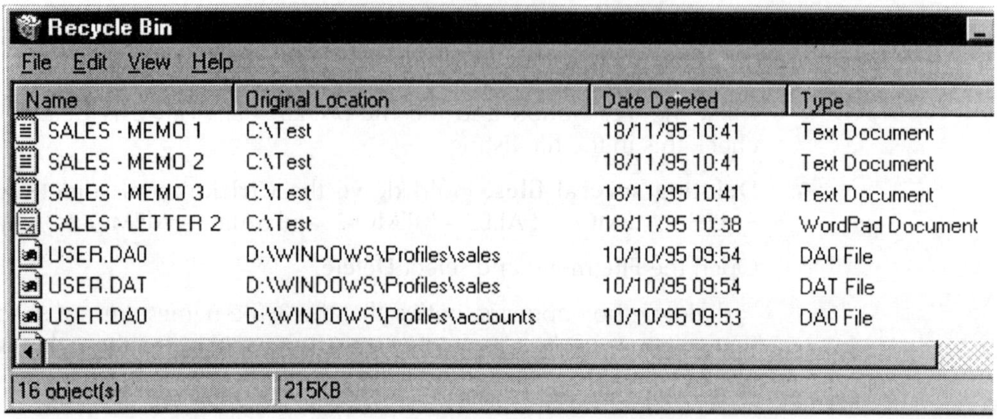

Figure 12

2. **Checking the size of the recycle bin.** Close the Recycle Bin window and then right click the Recycle Bin icon.

   Select **Properties** from the menu. A dialogue box appears.

Check that the **Global** tab is selected which determines the settings for all drives.
The default size of the recycle bin is 10% of total drive space.
Notice that there is also the option to delete files immediately, without moving them to the Recycle Bin.

Click the tabs for the other drives, they are set to 10% too.

There are no tabs for diskette drives, deleted files on diskette are deleted permanently unless you use the MS-DOS undelete command or another disk utility.

Close the Properties dialogue box.

3. **Deleting a file permanently.** Open the Recycle Bin window again and select one of the files.

   Choose **Delete** from the **File** menu. Confirm the deletion and the file is permanently deleted.

4. **Restoring a deleted file.** Select a file from the Recycle Bin.

   Choose **Restore** from the **File** menu. The file is restored to its original location in the Test folder.

5. **Clearing out the recycle bin.** There should be at least two files left in the Recycle Bin. *Check that there are no other files that you may wish to restore at a later date.*

   Open the **File** menu and select **Empty Recycle Bin**.

   Confirm the deletion and the bin is emptied.

6. Close the Recycle Bin.

   Carry straight on with the next activity.

Activity 9 Deleting folders

Folders can be deleted in the same ways as files, so all the operations learnt in the previous activity apply equally to folders. Folders deleted from hard disk, like files, can be undeleted. However you must take even more care as deleting a folder will delete any files and further subfolders it contains You must check the confirmation messages very carefully!

We will delete the Test folder and the remaining files it contains.

1. Open the Explorer Window and click the folder icon for the Test Folder once so that it is selected (highlighted).

   Open the **File** menu and select **Delete.**
   When the Confirm Folder Delete dialogue box appears check that the folder name Test is shown – see Figure 13. If so click the **Yes** button.

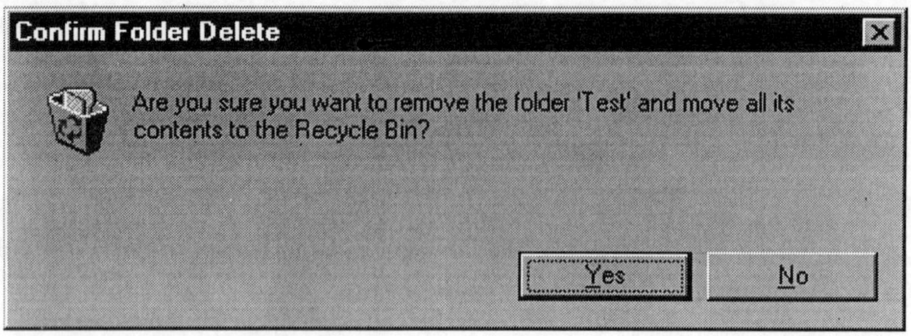

Figure 13

If any other name is shown then take the No option, select the correct folder and try again.

2. **Restoring a folder.** Now open the Recycle Bin and check the deleted files have been placed there.

   Restore one of the files and check the hard drive using Explorer. You will find that the Test folder has been restored and that it contains the restored file.

3. Delete the Test Folder again and empty the Recycle Bin.

4. **Independent activity.** Make sure that diskette a containing the practice files is in the diskette drive.

   Open Explorer if necessary and check that the main diskette drive window is selected, not a subfolder.

   Maximise the window.

   All files with SALES in the file name are now located in the Sales folder, all files with ACCOUNTS in the file name are located in the Accounts folder.

   All files not in these folders are duplicates of these and can be deleted. Do this.
   When you have done so check the Recycle Bin – none of the deleted files have been moved there. Deleted files on diskette cannot be recovered.

Summary of menu commands

Notes

Menu commands show the menu name first, followed by the command to choose from the menu, e.g. Edit-Clear means open the Edit menu and select the Clear command. Where a command is available from a particular window this is indicated in brackets.

(My Computer)

Edit-Copy	Select a file or folder for copying
Edit-Cut	Select a file or folder for moving
Edit-Paste	Copy/Move selected file or folder
File-Delete	Delete file or folder
File-New-Folder	Create new folder
File-Rename	Rename a file or folder
View-Options-Folder	Display/Do not display multiple windows
View-Refresh	Update display of files/folders

(Recycle Bin)

File-Empty Recycle Bin	Permanently delete files or folders
File-Restore	Restore a deleted file or folder

unit 6

More on disks and files

Introduction

In this unit you will be learning how to create a system disk, how to display hidden files, and how to associate a file with an application. There is a final independent activity which involves organising files into folders and subfolders.

Skills covered	Activity
Files – associating with an application	3
File Attributes – checking	2.3
Hidden Files – displaying	2
System Disk – creating	1

Previous skills required	covered in unit
Using the standard Windows components	1

Resources required

The two practice diskettes created in Unit 2 and 5, plus a further blank diskette

Activity 1 Creating a system disk

Windows 95 contains a number of key system files that are essential for your PC to start and to run. If they are accidentally removed, or damaged by a virus you will need a system disk to start or 'boot up' your computer.

You can transfer the key system files to diskette using the My Computer application. These files will allow the system to re-start. One can either add the system files when formatting a disk – see Unit 3 , Activity 1 – or at a later stage as we are doing now. We will use the practice diskette b created in the previous unit that is already formatted but any disk will do.

Note: One only needs one system disk; It is not necessary to copy system files onto diskettes only used to store files.

1. Insert the diskette and open the My Computer window.

   Single click the icon for the diskette drive to select it – do not double click it to open the window – *a disk cannot be formatted when its window is open.*

2. Open the **File** menu and select **Format.** A dialogue box **Format – 3 1/2 Floppy (A:)** is displayed. As the disk is already formatted we will not format it as it would erase the backup files.

3. Select the option **Copy system files only.**

   Click the **Start** button.

   When complete click the **Close** button and continue with the next activity.

Activity 2 Displaying hidden files

Normally you can view all the files on disk using My Computer or Explorer. However, some files are always hidden to protect them from interference, notably some of the the key system files mentioned in the previous activity. It is essential that these files are not deleted or renamed, otherwise the computer will not run properly. Hiding files that are not normally moved or deleted also reduces the size of the display. Sometimes it is useful to check that these hidden files are on your system disk.

1. Insert the system disk that you created in the last activity if necessary.

   Call up **My Computer** if necessary and double click the diskette drive icon.

   The file COMMAND is listed; this is the command processor program that executes key MS-DOS commands.

   Two more files may also be displayed in the drive window, IO.SYS and MS-DOS.SYS

   The .SYS extension identifies them as system files.

   If they are *not* displayed then proceed to section 2.

2. Open the **View** menu and select **Options.** A dialogue box appears.

   Click the **View** tab at the top of the window, the files that are normally not shown are listed.

   Select the **Show all files** option.

   Click **OK.**

3. To find out more about the two system files right click the file name and select **Properties** from the menu.

A dialogue box appears – make sure that the **General** tab is selected.

The final section of the dialogue box lists the file attributes – r, h, s and a:

Read-only – the file is protected from amendment – it can be read but not written to,

Hidden – the file is not normally listed in Explorer,

System file – it is part of the computer's operating system,

Archive – this attribute is used with certain programs to control whether a file is backed up. Once a file has been backed up its archive 'flag' is set off; this is checked by a backup program and it is not included in the next back up. If the file is changed the archive flag is set on again.

4. Now we will hide these two files.

   Follow the steps in section 2, to deselect the **Show all Files** option.

   Only the COMMAND file is now displayed in the drive window. IO.SYS and MSDOS.SYS are hidden.

5. **A final warning.** Do not list hidden files on a regular basis. They are hidden to prevent their being deleted, re-named or moved. It is all too easy to do this particularly if you are selecting blocks of files. Similarly do not hide regular files – you may forget where you have hidden them!

Activity 3 Associating a file with an application

In MS-DOS and earlier versions of Windows a file name could only consist of up to 8 characters, plus an optional extension of up to three characters, separated from the filename by a full stop or 'dot'. Windows 95 allows file names of up to 255 characters.

Extensions are still used by Windows 95 to associate a type of file with a particular application but the extension is normally hidden from the user. This association saves time when you want to retrieve a file; you have no need to start the application and then open the file – opening the file automatically starts the associated application. If data files are *not* given the standard default extension then Windows cannot automatically associate them with the software package (i.e. the program) that created them. This means that when you try to open the file by double clicking the icon, eg in Explorer, you will get an error message. In this case you must tell Windows which program is associated with the data file.

If you have a set of files which share a non-standard extension you can create your own association.

1. Make sure that diskette a containing the practice files is inserted in the diskette drive, open Explorer and check that the diskette window is selected.

Maximise the window.

2. Open the Sales Folder and double click the file SALES – LETTER 2. The Wordpad application starts automatically. Windows can associate the file with the Wordpad application program that was used to created it.

Exit from the document back to Explorer – the file and its associated program is closed.

3. Now open the **View** menu and select **Options.**

A dialogue box appears. Find the option:

Hide MS-DOS file extension for file types that are registered.

This option is normally selected so that file types 'known' or registered with Windows 95 do not display their extensions.

Deselect this option and click the **OK** button.

4. The practice files are now shown with their extension – see Figure 1 – you may have to widen the Name column to see them. (drag the column divider)

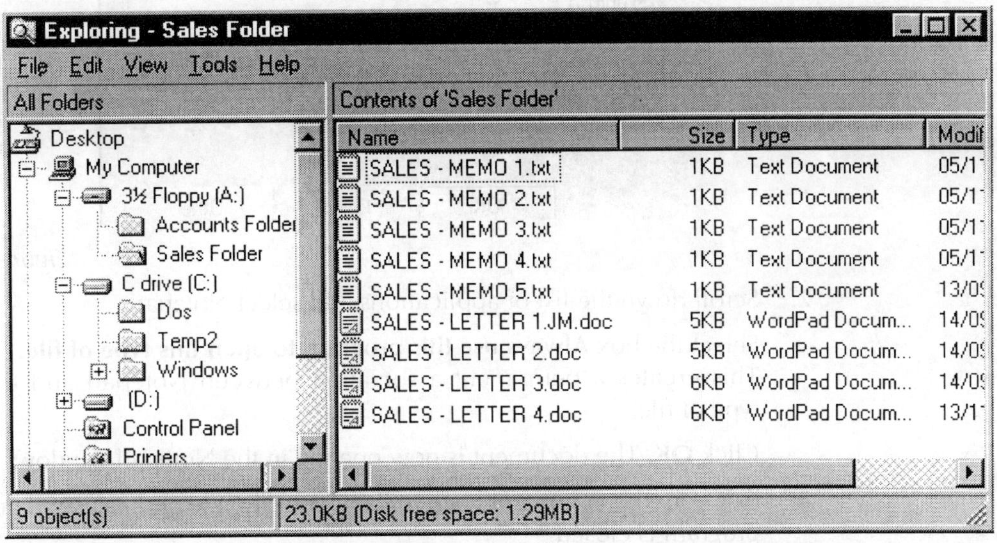

Figure 1

The sample files that you created are all short data files, they contain text – mainly alphabetic characters and numbers. The files created in Notepad, the Windows text editor, have the extension .TXT automatically assigned to them; files with the extension .DOC were created in Wordpad, the Windows word processor.

5. Select the file SALES – MEMO 1.txt – do not open it.

Open the File menu and select **Rename.**

Change the extension to **.JMM** – the file is renamed ACCOUNTS – MEMO1.JMM

Click elsewhere on the window – a dialogue box appears warning you that the file may become unusable. Click the **Yes** button.
The file is now renamed – notice that the design of the icon has changed as Windows no longer associates it with any application.

6. Double click the renamed file to open it.
The **Open as** dialogue box appears – see Figure 2. You are being asked to associate the file with a registered Windows application.

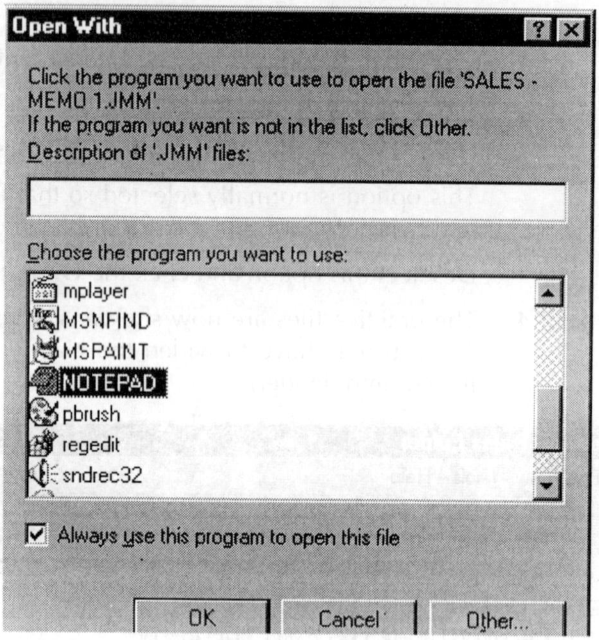

Figure 2

7. Scroll down the list of applications and select Notepad.

Select the box **Always use this program to open this type of file.** This creates a permanent association between Notepad and this type of file.

Click **OK.** The document is now opened in the Notepad window.

8. Exit from the document back to Explorer – the file and its associated program is closed.
Windows can now associate the file ACCOUNTS – MEMO 1.JMM with the Notepad application. To make this point open and close it again.

9. Hide the file name extensions by repeating step 3 above and deselecting the option:

Hide MS-DOS file extension for file types that are registered.

Activity 4 Independent activity

Your practice files are now stored in two folders – **Sales** and **Accounts.** They consist of two file types – see previous activity.

Create two further subfolders within each folder called **Memos** and **Letters.**

Move all files with the word **letters** in their file name to subfolder **Letters**

Move all files with the word **memos** in their file name to the sub folder **Memos.**

The final structure will be as follows:

- Sales Folder
  - Memos
    - SALES – MEMO 1
    - SALES – MEMO 2
    - SALES – MEMO 3
    - SALES – MEMO 4
  - Letters
    - SALES – LETTER 1.JM
    - SALES – LETTER 2
    - SALES – LETTER 3
    - SALES – LETTER 4
- Accounts Folder
  - Memos
    - ACCOUNTS – MEMO 1
    - ACCOUNTS – MEMO 2
    - ACCOUNTS – MEMO 3
    - ACCOUNTS – MEMO 4
  - Letters
    - ACCOUNTS – LETTER 1
    - ACCOUNTS – LETTER 2
    - ACCOUNTS – LETTER 3
    - ACCOUNTS – LETTER 4

Hint: To create a folder within another folder you will need to open the Accounts and the Sales folders before taking the **File – New – Folder** option.

Summary of menu commands

Notes

Menu commands show the menu name first, followed by the command to choose from the menu, e.g. Edit-Clear means open the Edit menu and select the Clear command. Where a command is available from a particular window this is indicated in brackets.

(My Computer)

File-Format	Format/Create system diskette
File-Rename	Rename a file or folder
View-Options-View	Show/Hide various file types/file details

unit 7

Customising your system

Introduction

Windows 95 lets you create various types of shortcut to applications that you use frequently. You can create shortcut icons on the desktop and use them to start applications or open folders, you can have applications start up as soon as you start Windows and you can send documents direct to the printer by 'dropping' them into a special print folder.

Skills covered	Activity
Files – associating with an application	3
Print Jobs – changing	5.6
Print Queue – creating	5.5
Shortcut to application – creating	1
Shortcut to Folder – creating	2, 3
Shortcut to Printer – creating	5
Shortcut Wizard – using	1
Startup Application – creating	4
Startup Application – removing	4.10

Previous skills required	covered in unit
Using the standard Windows components	1

Resources required

The diskette with the practice files created in Unit 2

Activity 1 Creating a shortcut to a program

The standard way of starting a program is to open a series of menus and windows using the Start button, Explorer or My Computer. Windows 95 allows you bypass these steps by creating shortcut icons on the desktop. Let's try this for the Wordpad and Paint applications.

1. First we need to open the folder which contains the Wordpad application.

Click the **Start** button. Select the **Programs** then the **Windows Explorer** option.

Adjust the size of the window if necessary so that part of the desktop is visible. The various drive icons are displayed in the left hand side of the Window.

Double click the drive icon that contains the **Windows** folder – usually drive C or D if your PC is not networked.

Check for the Program Files folder in the right hand window – see Figure 1. If you can't find it explore another disk drive.

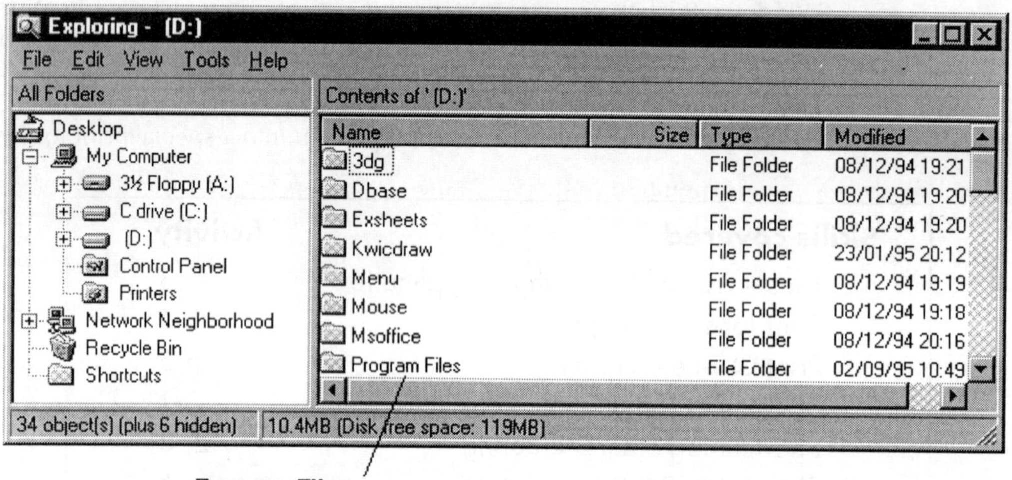

Figure 1

2. Double click the **Program Files** subfolder.

   Within the Program Files subfolder are more subfolders – open the **Accessories** subfolder.
   Various application icons are displayed, including Wordpad – see Figure 2.

3. Use the mouse to drag the Wordpad icon onto the desktop.

   Release the mouse button.

4. A new icon appears on the desk top **Shortcut to Wordpad.** If a menu appears select the option **Create Shortcut(s) here.**

   Double click the icon and the Wordpad program starts. This is a much faster way of starting the application than using a series of windows and menus.

   Note: Right clicking the shortcut icon displays a menu allowing you to delete, rename and copy the shortcut. The Properties option also allows you to select another icon for the shortcut.

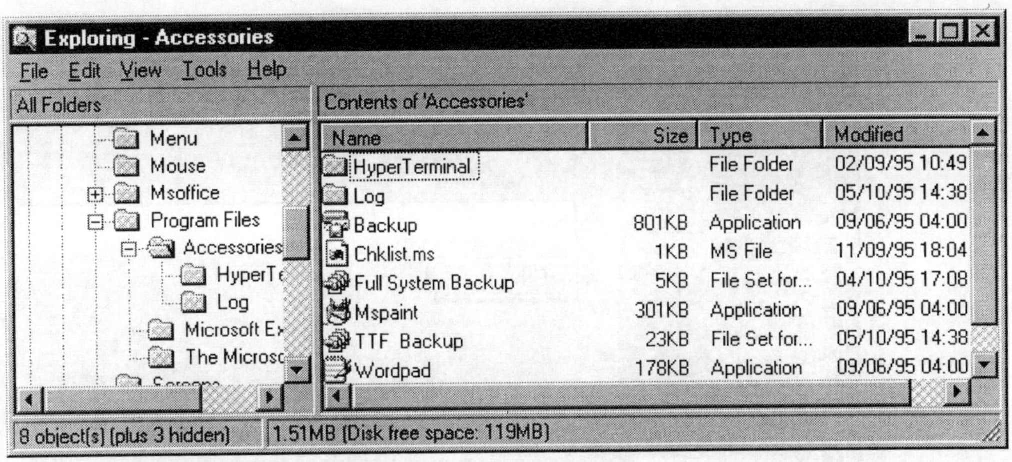

Figure 2

5. **Independent activity.** Create a desktop shortcut for the Notepad program. It is in the Windows folder. Rename it 'Start Notepad'

6. **Using shortcut wizard.** Shortcut Wizard makes creating a shortcut even easier. (a *wizard* is a series of dialogue boxes guiding you the steps of a process and is used extensively in Microsoft applications)

7. Insert practice disk a in the diskette drive.

   Right click anywhere on the desktop – a menu opens.

   Select the **New** then the **Shortcut** option.

8. The Create Shortcut dialogue box is displayed – see Figure 3.

9. You can create a shortcut to a file or to a drive as well as a program. We'll do this for the diskette drive.

   Enter the drive reference letter in the command line box, eg **a:** or **b:**, and click the **Next** button.

   The next dialogue box appears asking you to name the shortcut. Enter the name **Select Drive A** and click the **Finish** button.
   The shortcut icon appears on the desktop. Now double click the icon to test it

Activity 2 Creating a shortcut to a folder

In the previous activity we created a shortcut to a program and a drive. In this activity we'll create a shortcut to folder on diskette. (obviously it will only work if the correct diskette is inserted in the drive)

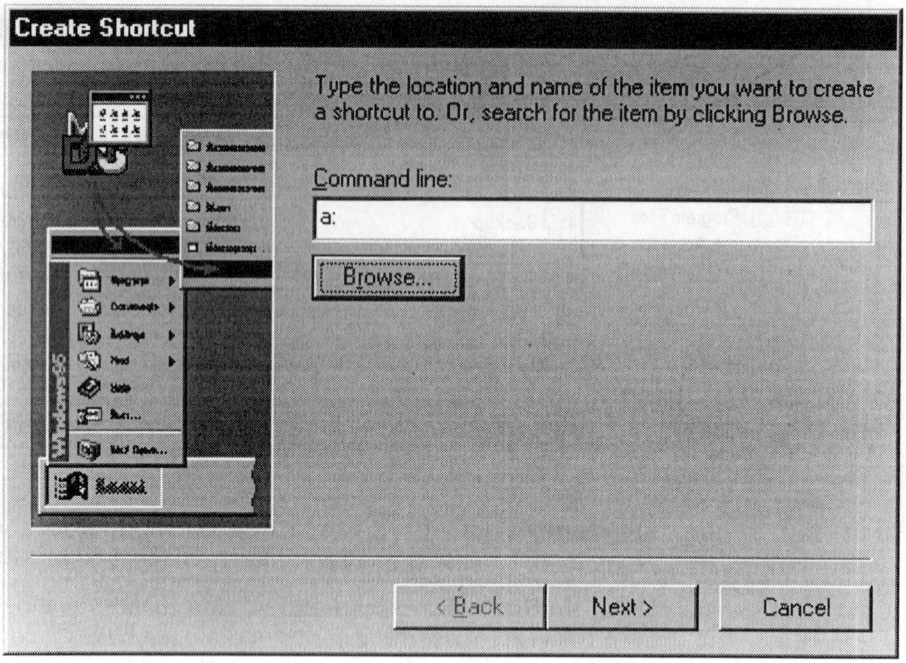

Figure 3

1. Insert practice disk a in the diskette drive.

   If necessary start Explorer again – click the **Start** button,select the **Programs** then the **Windows Explorer** options.

2. Double click the diskette drive icon and identify the **Sales** Folder.

   Move the cursor onto the Sales Folder icon, hold the *right hand* mouse button down and drag the icon onto the desktop.

   Release the mouse button and a menu appears. Select the option **Create Shortcut(s) here.**

3. A new icon appears on the desk top **Shortcut to Sales Folder.** (it can be deleted, renamed etc as before, by right clicking the icon)

   Double click on the icon and the Sales Folder window opens, displaying the files that it contains.

   Close the window

4. **Independent activity.** You also have an Accounts Folder on your practice diskette. Create a shortcut to this folder too.

Activity 3 Creating a shortcut folder

We now have five shortcut icons on the desktop – see Figure 4.

To reduce clutter they can be placed in a folder.

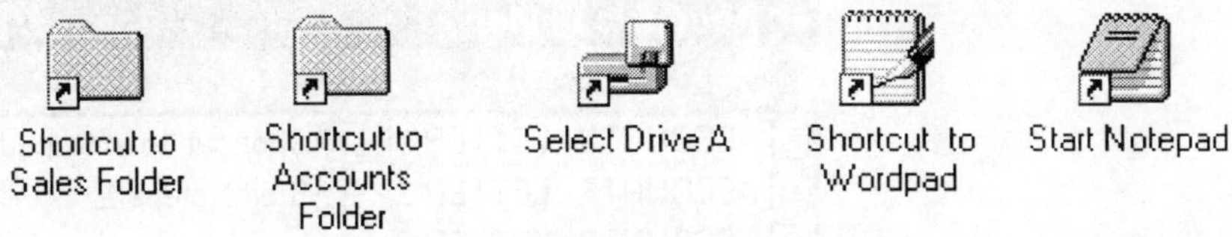

Figure 4

1. Right click anywhere on the desktop – a menu opens.

   Select the **New** then the **Folder** option.

   Rename the folder **Shortcuts.**

   Now use the left mouse button to drag the shortcuts into the folder.

2. Double click the folder – the window shows the shortcuts – see Figure 5.

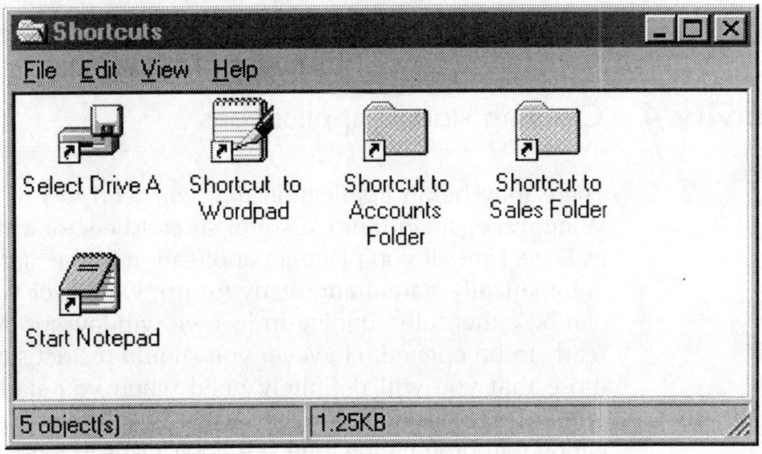

Figure 5

3. **Independent activity.** A copy of a shortcut can be placed at any other useful point, eg in a drive or folder to provide shortcuts. For example the Sales Folder and Accounts Folder on your practice diskette are used to store letters created in Wordpad and memos created in Notepad. It will be useful to have short cuts to these two applications if we want to create any new documents.

   Open **My Computer** and display the window for the diskette drive.

   Use the left mouse button to drag copies of the Notepad and Wordpad Shortcuts to the Accounts Folder then the Sales Folder.

   Open the destination folder to check that they have been copied – they should resemble Figure 6.

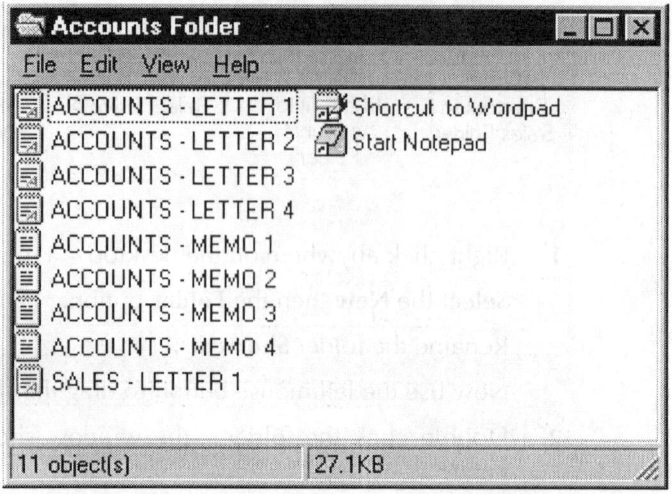

Figure 6

Activity 4 Creating startup applications

There may be an application that you tend to use when you first start Windows eg a word processor or spreadsheet, or a Windows utility such as Date/Time. If you place an application in the Startup Folder it will be automatically started and ready for use whenever you start Windows. It can be either fully running in its own window, or displayed as an icon, ready to be opened. However you should restrict startup applications to those that you will definitely need when you start Windows; it takes time to load up individual applications and therefore any startup application will prolong the time Windows takes to load.

As an example we will place Notepad in the Startup Folder.

1. Click the **Start** button, then select the **Settings** and the **Taskbar** options.

   When the dialogue box appears click the **Start Menu Programs** tab.

2. **Finding the application.** Click the **Add** button which calls up the Shortcut wizard – see Activity 1 above.

   To type the name of the program that you want to start directly in the Command line box requires that you give the path, eg **C:\windows\notepad.exe** which involves some knowledge of MS-DOS commands. If you prefer click the **Browse** button then proceed as follows:

   The Browse dialogue box appears.
   First make sure that the drive that contains the Windows folder is displayed in the Look in: box, if not click the down arrow and select it – see Figure 7.

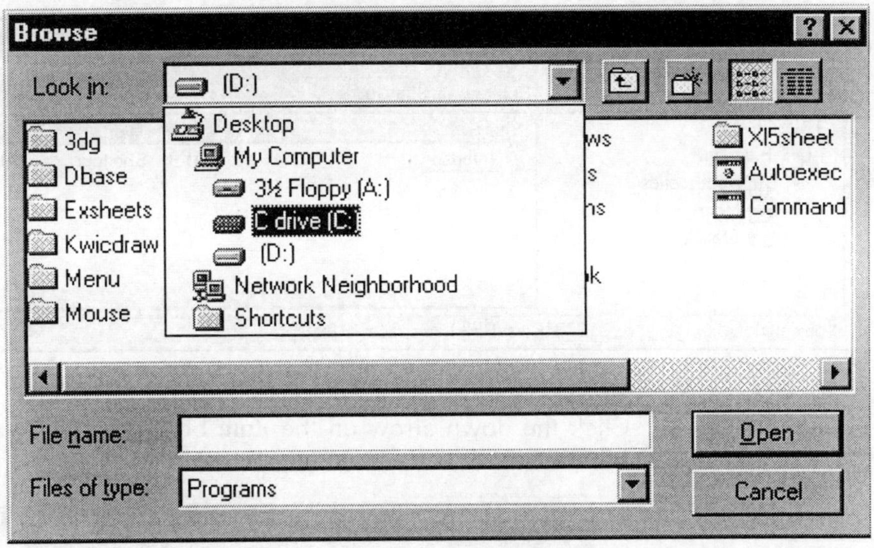

Figure 7

Find the **Windows** folder in the window display and double click it.

Find the **Notepad** icon in the next window display and double click it.
You are returned to the Browse dialogue box and the Command line box is now complete, eg C:\WINDOWS\NOTEPAD.EXE

3. Click the **Next** button and the **Select Program Folder** window is displayed.

   Click the **Startup** folder icon then the **Next** button.

4. On the final dialogue box you can rename the shortcut; accept the default offered and click the **Finish** button.

5. You are returned to the Taskbar Properties dialogue box. We will start Notepad as an icon on the taskbar rather than an open window.
   Click the **Advanced** button.

6. An Explore window for the Start menu is displayed – double click the folder icon if necessary.

   Click the (+) sign next to the **Programs** folder to expand it.

   Click the **StartUp** folder to open it – the Notepad shortcut icon is displayed in the right window – see Figure 8.

7. Right click the **Notepad** icon – a menu appears.
   Select the **Properties** option.
   The Notepad Properties dialogue box appears. Make sure the **Shortcut** tab is selected.

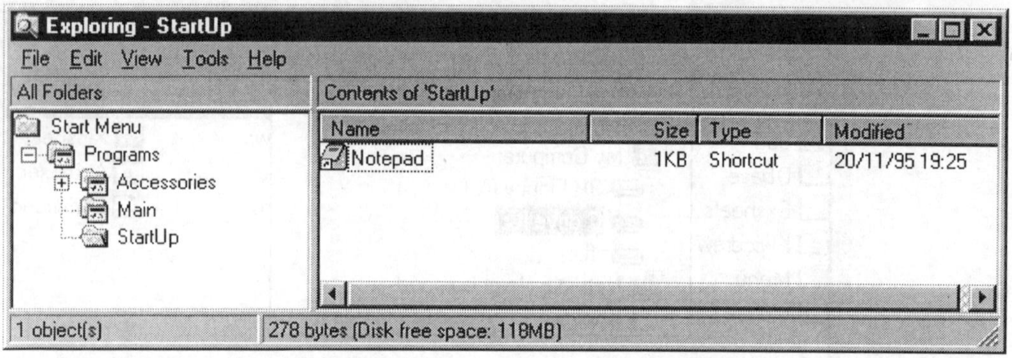

Figure 8

8. Click the down arrow on the **Run:** box – see Figure 9. and select **Minimized.**

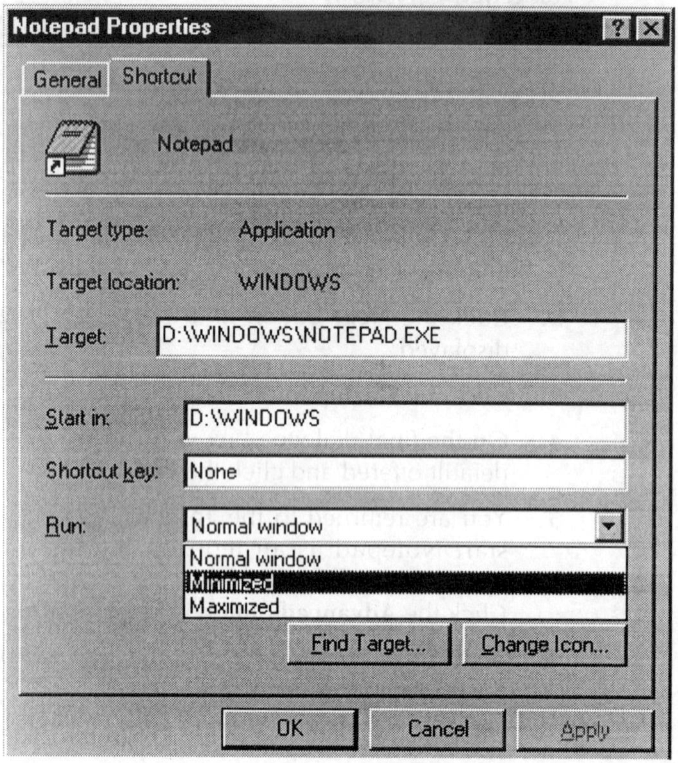

Figure 9

Click the **OK** button.

Finally close any dialogue boxes remaining open.

9. **Testing the startup application.** Exit from Windows and Re-start it. The Notepad icon should start up automatically as an icon on the taskbar.

10. Add the Paint application to the Startup menu.

11. **Removing an option from the startup menu.** This is simply a matter of repeating step 1 above then clicking the Remove button. You may wish to remove Notepad from the Startup folder if you are sharing your PC with others who do not need this option.

12. **Independent activity.** You can also use these techniques to add or remove any option from the Start menu. Add the Paint program to the Start (not the Startup) menu following steps 1 – 4 above. If you are successful the Start menu will offer it as an extra option when the Start button is clicked.

    Check that the option works then remove it from the Start menu.

Activity 5 Customising printing

The usual way to print is to open the document and select the Print option from the File menu. Instead you can create a print shortcut on the desktop and print by dragging the document icon onto it. You can also form a print queue by dragging several documents.

1. Open the **My Computer** window and double click the **Printers** folder.

2. Right click the printer icon, hold the mouse button down and drag the icon onto the desktop.

   Release the mouse button and a menu appears. Select the option **Create Shortcut(s) here.**

3. A new object appears on the desk top **Shortcut to [...your printer].** You can rename the icon by right clicking it if you wish.

4. **Printing a single document.** Insert practice disk a in the diskette drive.

   In the My Computer window double click the diskette drive icon.

   Use the mouse to drag a text document from the diskette window on top of the printer shortcut icon. The document will open and print (one copy only)

5. **Printing several documents.** This can be useful when you are away from the computer. It is possible to check or change the status of print jobs when printing has started.

   When you have finished this section continue with the next section as quickly as possible before printing is complete.

   Hold down the **Ctrl** key and select four Wordpad documents in the My Computer window.

   Keep the Ctrl key pressed down, locate the cursor anywhere on the group of documents and drag them on top of the printer shortcut icon.

   Release the mouse then the Ctrl key.

A dialogue box appears asking you to confirm that you are trying to print multiple documents:
Click **Yes** and the Wordpad application opens. The documents to be printed appears as buttons on the task bar.

6. **Changing print jobs**. Before the first document starts printing double click the printer shortcut icon. A printer window opens, displaying the remaining documents to be printed – see Figure 10.

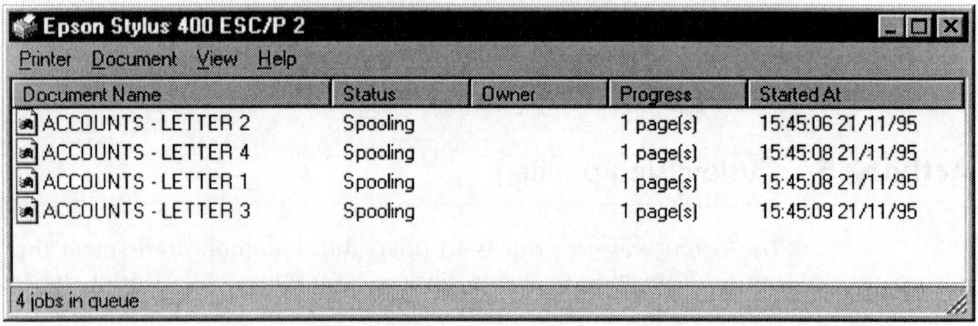

Document Name	Status	Owner	Progress	Started At
ACCOUNTS - LETTER 2	Spooling		1 page(s)	15:45:06 21/11/95
ACCOUNTS - LETTER 4	Spooling		1 page(s)	15:45:08 21/11/95
ACCOUNTS - LETTER 1	Spooling		1 page(s)	15:45:08 21/11/95
ACCOUNTS - LETTER 3	Spooling		1 page(s)	15:45:09 21/11/95

Figure 10

Open the **Printer** menu and select the **Pause Printing** option.

Note: All this may take a very long time, unless your PC is quite powerful as you are printing from diskette and each document must be opened and queued.

The printer window shows the progress of your printing jobs, the length of each document and the time it was started. The Owner column is useful if your printer is shared by several networked users.

7. **Changing the print queue order.** You can change the order of printing by dragging one document above another – try it. This will make you unpopular on a network and may not be available!

8. **Pausing an individual document.** Clicking the document to select it, then select **Pause Printing** from the **Document** menu. Try this – a message appears in the status column.
   Select this option again and the pause status is removed.

9. **Cancel one of the print jobs.** Select the document then choose **Cancel Printing** from the **Document** menu. The document is removed.

10. **Start or cancel all print jobs.**The Printer menu can be used to start all the print jobs again or to cancel (purge) them all. We will do the former.

    Open the **Printer** menu and select **Pause Printing** – it is de-selected and the remaining documents are printed.

11. Close the **Printer** window and the **My Computer** window.

12. **Printing using the send to option.** Click the **Start** button. Select the **Programs** then the **Windows Explorer** option. The various drive icons are displayed in the left hand window.

Adjust the size of the window if necessary so that the printer shortcut is visible on the desktop.

Double click the drive icon that contains the **Windows** folder – usually drive C or D if your PC is not networked.

Check for the Windows folder in the right hand window – see Figure 1 above. If you can't find it explore another disk drive.

Open the Windows folder.

13. Double click the **Send** to folder – the contents are displayed.

Right click the printer shortcut icon and drag it from the desktop to the Send to folder.

Release the mouse button and a menu is displayed – select the **Create Shortcut Here** option. The printer shortcut is copied into the **Send** to menu.

14. Double click the diskette drive icon in the left hand Explorer window to open it.

Right click any document in the right hand window and a menu appears. Select the **Send to** option.

Select the printer shortcut and the document is sent to the printer. If anything this is even more convenient than the 'drag and drop' method that we have just learned.

Summary of commands

Note

Commands show the object to select first, followed by the command to choose from the menu, e.g. Start Button-Help means click the Start Button and select the Help command. Where a command is available from a particular window this is indicated in brackets.

Start-Programs-Windows Explorer	Start Windows Explorer
Start-Settings-Taskbar	Change Taskbar properties
(Windows Explorer)	
File-New-Shortcut	Create new shortcut
File-New-Folder	Create new folder

unit 8

Object linking and embedding

Introduction

More and more applications are Windows based – they use the features of the Windows graphical user interface (GUI for short). Once you have learned to use such features as the mouse, icons, windows, dialogue boxes and pull-down menus you can start to use any Windows application, eg a word processor, spreadsheet and database.

Users have also come to expect easy transfer of data between Windows applications; for example you may have created a graph using a spreadsheet and want to copy it into a word processed report. Also whenever the original graph changes you want the version in the report to be updated too – even though a word processor and a spreadsheet are completely different applications.

Microsoft (the producer of Windows) have created the standard for this to happen – OLE.

Skills covered	**Activity**
Files – associating with an application	3
Copying and pasting	1
Links – maintaining	3
Object Editing	1.8
Object Linking	2
Object Packaging	4

Previous skills required

Using the standard Windows components see Unit 1

Using Copy and Paste commands – see Unit 5, Activity 4

Resources required

The diskette with the practice files created in Unit 2 (or any other diskette)

Activity 1 Copying, pasting and embedding

1. **Copying and pasting.** Open the **Paint** application. It is part of the Accessories group.

   Produce the simple image shown in Figure 1. The exact shape and size do not matter, it is made up of an empty circle inside an empty rectangle. Drawing them is simply a matter of clicking the shape to select the tool, then dragging on the Paint screen to draw the shape – see Figure 2 if you have not used Paint before.

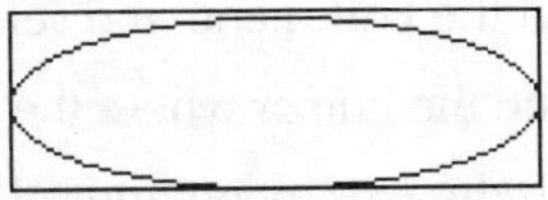

Figure 1

2. Enclose the image using the **Select** tool. (click the tool to select it, then drag to enclose the image)

   Open the **Edit** menu and select **Copy.**

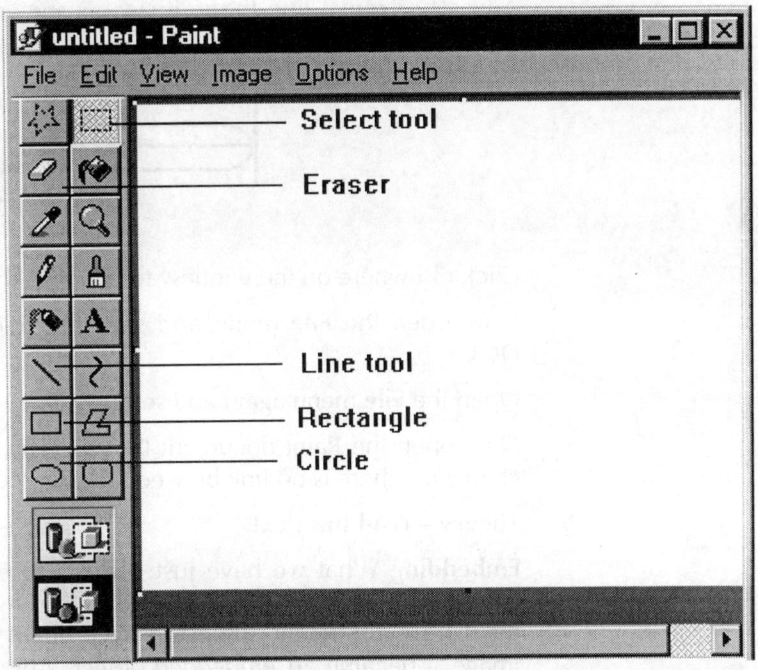

Figure 2

3. Save the Paint document on a diskette as IMAGE

4. Exit Paint and open **Wordpad.** It is part of the Accessories group.

   Type any few lines of text.

   Now open the **Edit** menu and select **Paste.** The image is pasted into the Wordpad document.

5. Minimise the Wordpad document and open the **Clipboard Viewer.** (it is part of the Accessories group) It contains the pasted image. Clipboard acts as the temporary storage area in main memory when data is cut or copied. It can only hold one chunk of data at a time, the next data to be copied or cut will overwrite the image.

6. **Object embedding.** Exit from the clipboard viewer and return to the Wordpad document.

   Click the image to select it – the image is surrounded by a rectangle.

7. Try copying and cutting the image within the document, ie:

   open the **Edit** menu and select **Cut** or **Copy,**

   locate the cursor where the image is to re-located,

   open the **Edit** menu and select **Paste.**

8. **In-place editing.** If you need to edit the image you can change back to its 'home' application – Paint – automatically

   Double-click the image – a Paint window opens, allowing you to edit the image.

   Add a horizontal line to the image as shown in Figure 3 – use the line tool.

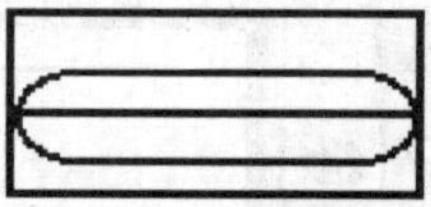

Figure 3

   Click elsewhere on the window to return to the Wordpad document.

   Now open the **File** menu and save the document on diskette as DOC1

   Open the **File** menu again and select **Exit**

   Now open the Paint document IMAGE. The original image has not changed – there is no link between the two.

9. **Theory – read this next.**

   Embedding What we have just done is to create information in a *'source'* document (Paint) and insert it into a *'destination'* document from a different application Wordpad) This information – the image – became an *embedded* object. Any changes can be made easily as an application window for the source application (Paint) opens automatically from within the destination document (Wordpad)

   When you embed an object in a document you **copy** the object from the source to the destination document. Once this happens the original and its copy cease to be linked in any way – editing the copy does not affect the original.

Activity 2 Object linking

Introduction

There are situations where you might want any changes to an original, eg a diagram or spreadsheet, to automatically update any copies of it that exist in other documents.

In this case you can create a *link* to the original. (you can link several documents to one original)

Not all Windows applications are capable of supporting Object Linking. Of those that do some may be capable of acting as the source or *'server'* application; others may only be capable of acting as the destination or *'client'* application.

In the examples that follow we use Paint as the server Application and Wordpad as the client application.

1. Open a new Paint document and create a simple map along the lines of Figure 4.

Figure 4

Hints: Use the Line tool for the road, the Rectangle tool for the building – see Figure 2 above if necessary.

When you use the Text tool you will need to drag a suitable sized box for the text first.

2. Save the Paint document onto diskette as MAP1

   Exit and close MAP1.

3. Open a new Wordpad document and type the following text:

   'Below is a map showing the new site for the university building.'

   Leave a couple of blank lines.

   Open the **Insert** menu and select **Object.**

   Click the **Create from File** button – the dialogue box changes to resemble Figure 5.

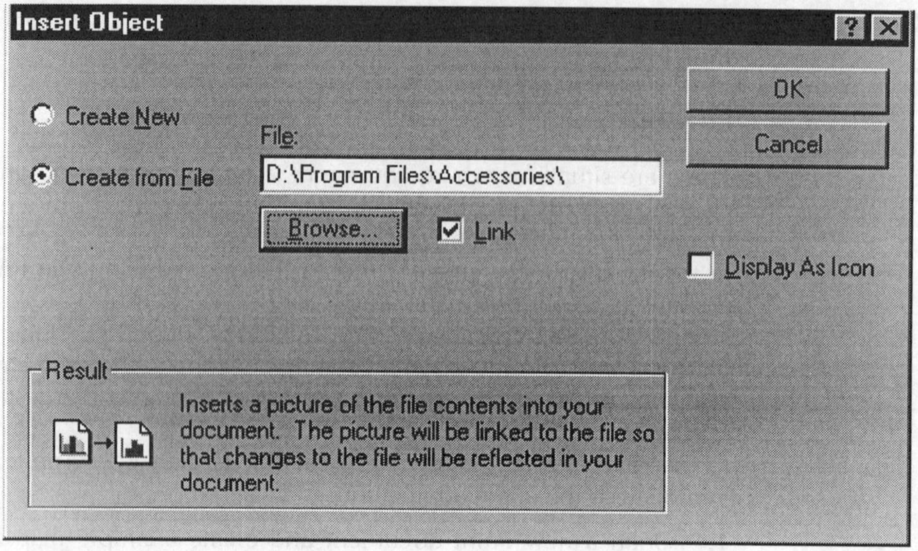

Figure 5

4. Click the **Link** box – this creates the link.

   Click the **Browse** button – we need to find the file MAP1.

   Make sure that the diskette drive is selected in the **Look in:** box.

   Select the MAP1 icon and click the **Insert** button.

   You are returned to the Insert Object dialogue box. Click **OK** and you are returned to the Wordpad document

5. The map is inserted in the wordpad document and is now linked to the original in the document MAP1
   Save the Wordpad document to diskette as DOC2

6. **Editing a linked drawing.** Double click on the map image, the Paint document MAP1 containing the original map image is opened.

   Arrange the Wordpad window and the Paint window so that the map image is visible in both documents. (drag the top window using the title bar)

   Amend the drawing by adding an IT Centre to the map as shown in Figure 6.

Figure 6

You will see both images are linked and change at the same time.

7. Open the **File** menu in the Paint window and choose **Save.** (this may take a long time as the links have to be saved too)

   Open the **File** menu in the Paint window and choose **Exit.**
   When you return to the Wordpad document DOC2 the linked image has also changed.

Activity 3 Maintaining links

The links that we have established so far mean that any updates to linked objects are automatic, however you can make the links manual so that you can choose whether the linked object gets updated. You can also break or delete links and fix broken links, eg if the name of a linked document is changed.

At the moment the linked object in the Wordpad document DOC2 is updated automatically. We can change this default so that the update in optional.

1. Make sure that DOC2 is open

   Right click anywhere on the map image – a menu appears.

   Select the **Object Properties** option.

   A dialogue box appears, select the **Link** tab.
   The link to the Paint document MAP1 is shown

   Click the **Update Manually** button.
   Click **OK.**

2. Now double click on the map image; the Paint document MAP1 containing the original map image is opened as before.

   Arrange the Wordpad window and the Paint window as before, so that the map image is visible in both documents.

   Amend the Paint image by removing the IT Centre from the map – use the Eraser tool. (see Figure 2 above if necessary)

   Open the **File** menu in the Paint window and choose **Save.**

   Open the **File** menu in the Paint window and choose **Exit.**

3. When you return to the Wordpad document DOC2 the linked image has not changed. This is because the link is now optional.

   To update the link repeat step 1, but this time click the **Update Now** button.

   Re-set the Update to **Automatic** then select **Close** – the link is updated and the IT Centre image is also removed from the linked Wordpad document DOC2.

4. End this activity by saving and closing the Wordpad document DOC2.
5. **Amending the original document.** A linked object can be worked on in both the client and the server application. In the previous activity we edited the map image from within the client application, Windows Wordpad. But we can just as easily do it from the server application, Windows Paint. As the object is shared rather than copied then all linked client documents will change as well.
6. Open the Paint document MAP1 and make a change to the map image.

   Save the changes and exit the document
   If the link is set to automatic – see previous activity – then the linked document will also be updated.
7. Now open the linked Wordpad document DOC2 – you will find that the map is updated.

   End this activity by closing all Wordpad and Paint documents.

Activity 4 Object packaging

Introduction

You now know how to link or embed objects from one application to another – OLE. You can also represent a linked object as an icon. Clicking the icon calls up the object so it can be viewed or edited. This has many uses, eg, the user can call up additional text, such as a note, diagram or a definition, if he wants to refer to it. Windows Help uses this idea a lot, clicking on a keyword or icon displays further help text. You can also package an application as an icon so that it can be executed by clicking the icon. In the next activity we will create an icon that calls up the calculator. As with OLE, not every Windows application will necessarily support this feature.

1. Start **Explorer** and double click the drive icon containing the Windows folder.

   Open the Windows folder and locate the **Packager** application.

   Open it – an Object Packager window is displayed.

   Open the **Edit** menu and select **Command Line** – a dialogue box is displayed.
2. Enter the command: **C:\WINDOWS\CALC.EXE** (this assumes that you have windows installed on C drive – make sure that you use the colon and the backslash characters when entering this command)

   Click the **OK** button – the command will now appear in the **Content** window – see Figure 7.

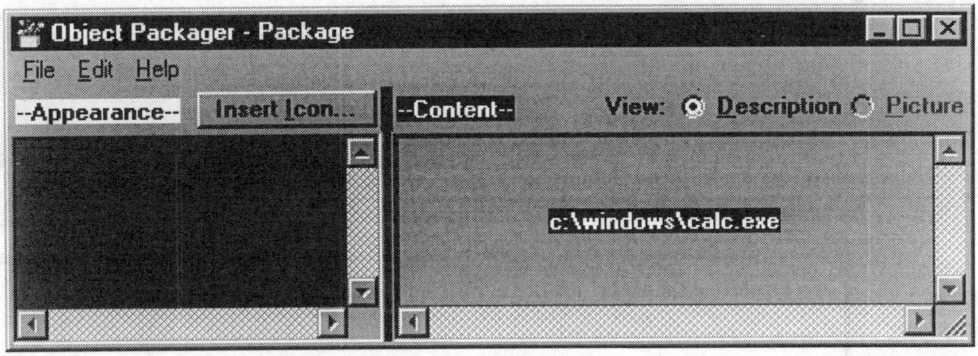

Figure 7

3. Now click the **Insert Icon** button – a group of icons appears Select a suitable one to represent your calculator.

   Click **OK** – it is shown in the **Appearance** window.

4. Open the **Edit** menu and select **Label.**

   Enter the label 'Calculate' in the dialogue box and click **OK** The icon is now labelled – see Figure 8.

   Open the **Edit** menu and select **Copy Package** (not Copy).

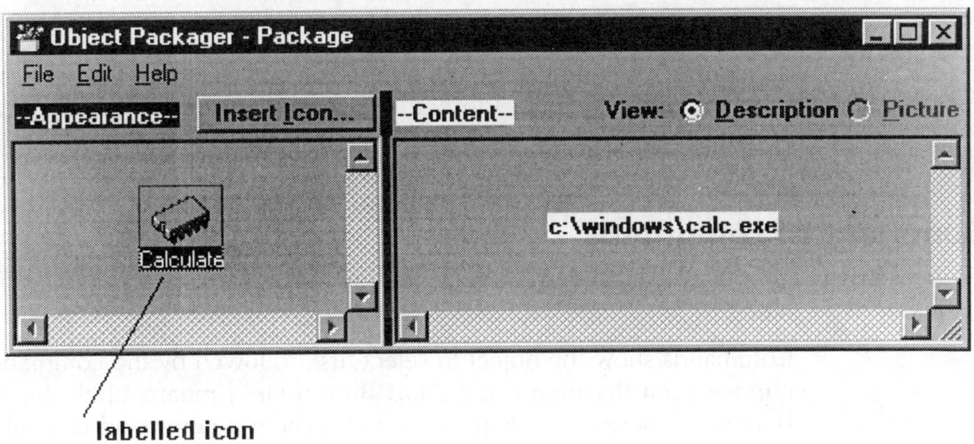

Figure 8

5. Now open a new Wordpad document and type the text;

   'If you want to use the calculator, double click the icon below'

   Now open the **Edit** menu and select **Paste.** The icon appears – see Figure 9.

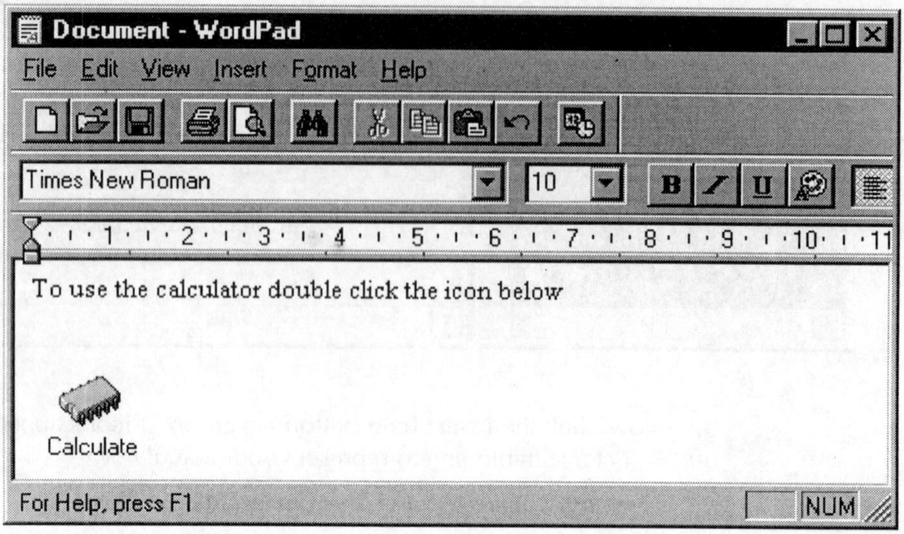

Figure 9

6. Now test the icon by double clicking it – it should call up the calculator – close it.

   Save the document to diskette as CALCULATOR and exit.

7. Close the Object Packager window.

8. **Note:** The icon can be edited if necessary by right clicking it, then choosing Package Object – Edit Package from the menu that appears.

Summary of commands

Note

Commands show the object to select first, followed by the command to choose from the menu, e.g. Start Button-Help means click the Start Button and select the Help command. Where a command is available from a particular window this is indicated in brackets.

Edit – Copy	Copy selected section onto the Clip board
Edit – Links	Maintain links between linked documents
Edit – Paste	Insert copied section into document
Insert-Object	Insert object into document from another file
(Object Packager)	
Edit-Command Line	Create MS-DOS command to package
Edit-Label	Edit the label of an icon
Edit-Copy Package	Copy Package onto clipboard

unit 9

Backing up and checking your system

Introduction

In this final unit we will be creating backups of files and using the important disk utilities Defragment, DriveSpace and ScanDisk. We will also check the your system's hardware components.

Skills covered	**Activity**
Device Manager – using	4
Disk – checking	2
Disk – compressing	3
Disk – defragmenting	2.5
Disk – scanning for Errors	2.4
Files – backing up	1
Files – restoring	1.10
Hardware – checking	4

Previous skills required

Using the standard Windows components see Unit 1

Resources required

Practice diskettes a and b

Activity 1 Backing up your data

You already know how to copy files from one diskette to another and from hard disk to diskette. (see Unit 5) However to protect the programs and data on your PC you need to establish organised backup procedures. The hard drive or a diskette may fail, you may lose a box of diskettes, or the whole PC may break down.

The cost to you (or your business) of lost data may be enormous, far exceeding the costs of the disks or hardware.

There are various backup methods, eg a regular backup of all files or an incremental backup of only those files that have changed. Often more than one set of backups are kept of different 'generations' .

It is good policy to store the backups securely at a different location to the originals.

The backup media will vary depending on your needs and resources. Backup to diskettes is still widely used but the increasing size of data and program files on hard disk make this increasingly impractical. Backup to tape is increasingly used by business and home users for mass offline storage. Backup to another hard disk is often used on networked PC's.

The Windows 95 Backup utility allows you define and save a backup set as a special file that defines which sets of files you want to back up; this file can then be run whenever you want to repeat the backup.

1. Click the **Start** Button, then select **Programs** then **Accessories** and **System Tools.**

   Backup should be located in this folder – see Figure 1.

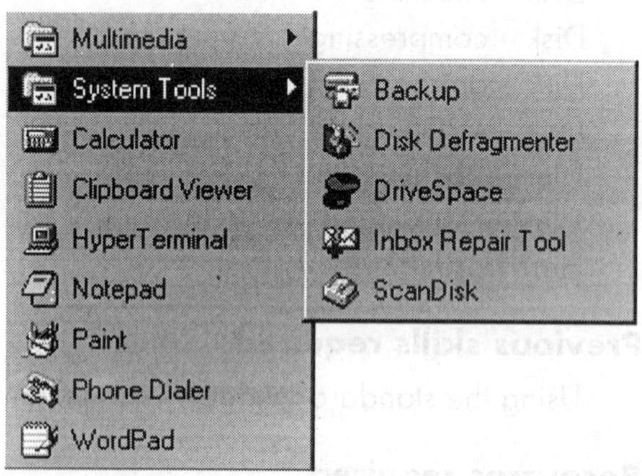

Figure 1

   Double click the icon to open the Backup application.

   The first time you start Backup you see a Welcome screen. Click **OK.**

   Note: If you cannot find Backup it may not have been installed. If you have access to the Windows 95 installation diskettes or CD-ROM then proceed as follows (otherwise omit this activity or seek help):

   Click the **Start** button, then **Settings** and **Control Panel.**

   Double click the **Add/Remove Programs** icon.

   Click the **Windows Setup** tab then the **Disk Tools** option.

   Click the **OK** button and from then on follow the instructions.

2. The Backup window opens. Backup automatically creates a full file backup and displays a dialogue box. Click **OK** and the Backup window is displayed – see Figure 2. Make sure that the **Backup** tab is selected.

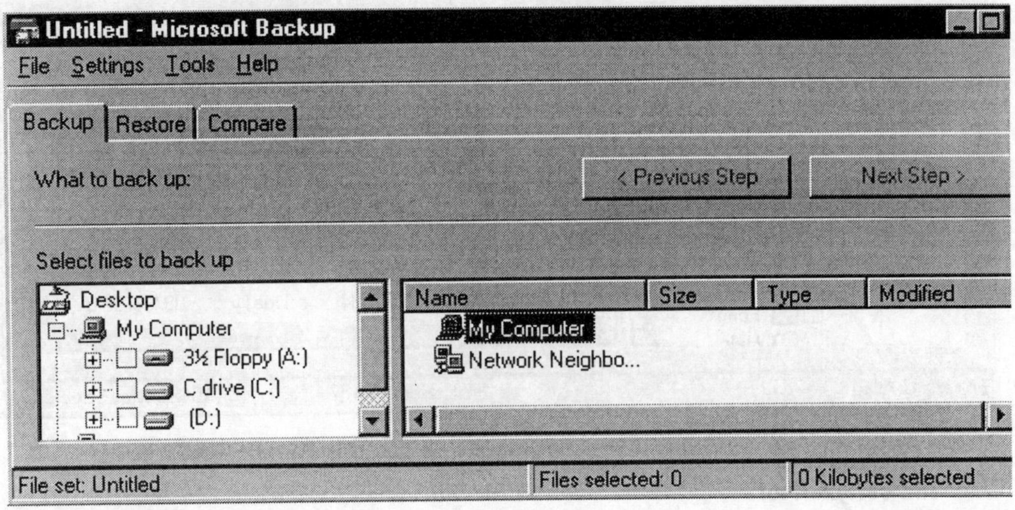

Figure 2

In the left hand window are the drives for your PC, the display is similar to the Explorer window. Next to each drive icon is the usual plus sign to display the folders, plus a checkbox which you click to include the drive in the backup.

3. As an example we will back up the Fonts subfolder in the Windows folder.

   Click the + sign next to the drive icon that holds the **Windows** folder – the folders are displayed in the left hand window.

   Double click the Windows folder in order to display its contents.

   Identify the **Fonts** folder and double click to open it.

   Click the check box next to the Fonts folder icon in the left hand window to include it in the backup – the window will now resemble Figure 3.

4. At the moment all the files in the Fonts folder are selected for backup. Let's filter out certain ones.

   First click the check box next to the Fonts folder again to deselect it.

   Open the **Settings** menu and select **File Filtering.** A dialogue box opens. We can choose to select files either by date or by file type.

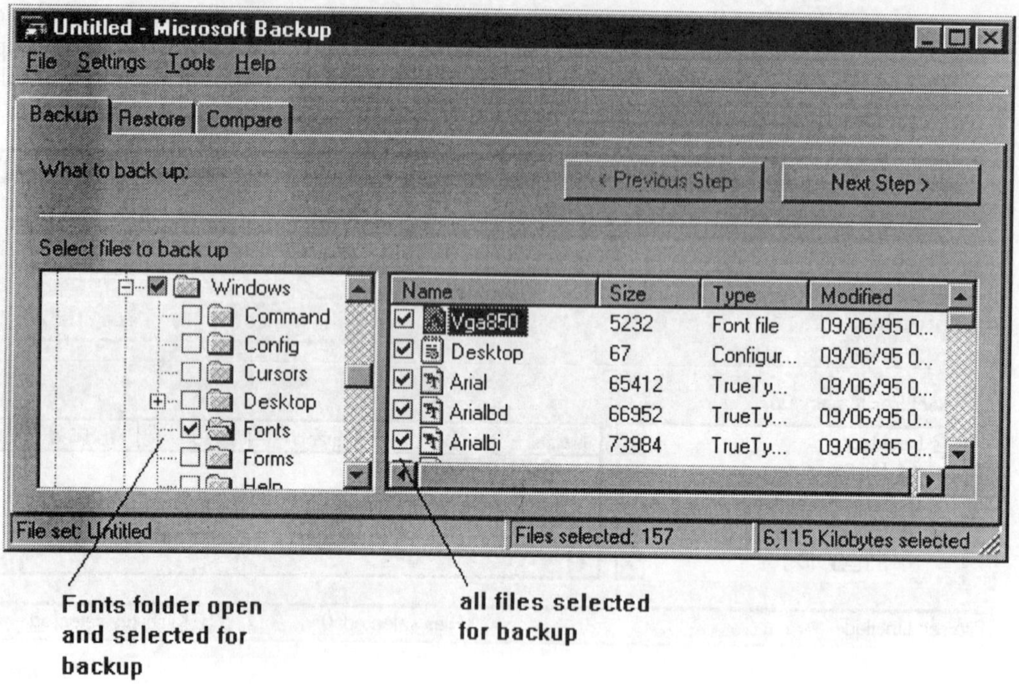

Figure 3

As an illustration we will exclude the Font files and the True Type font files.

5. Scroll through the **File types** list and select **(.Fon) File** and **(.ttf) TrueType Font File.**

   Click the **Exclude** then the **OK** button – see Figure 4.
   The Backup window is displayed again and only a few files are now shown to be included in the backup.

   Note: If the wrong files are selected select the File Filtering option again, click the Delete button and try again.

6. Now click the check boxes next to the remaining files – see Figure 5.
   Press the **Next Step>** button to take you to the second dialogue box.

7. You can now choose a destination for your backup. We will use practice diskette b.
   Insert it in the disk drive now. Now select the diskette drive icon in the left hand window.

8. **Backup options.** Open the **Settings** menu and select **Options.** Make sure that the **Backup** tab is selected.
   The dialogue box offers various options, let's review them:

   Type of Backup. The default is a full backup, ie all files selected – keep this selection.

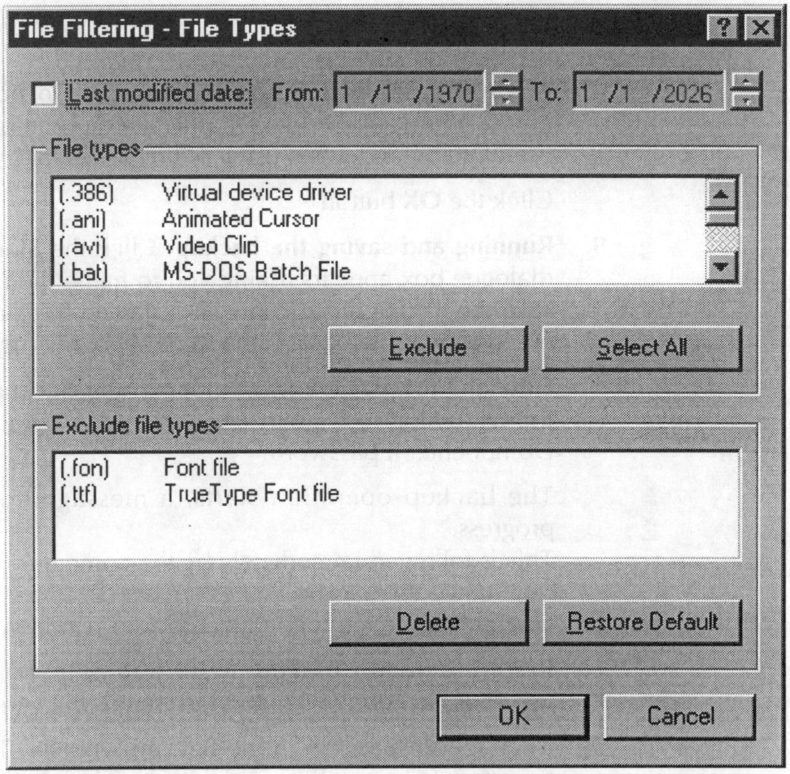

Figure 4

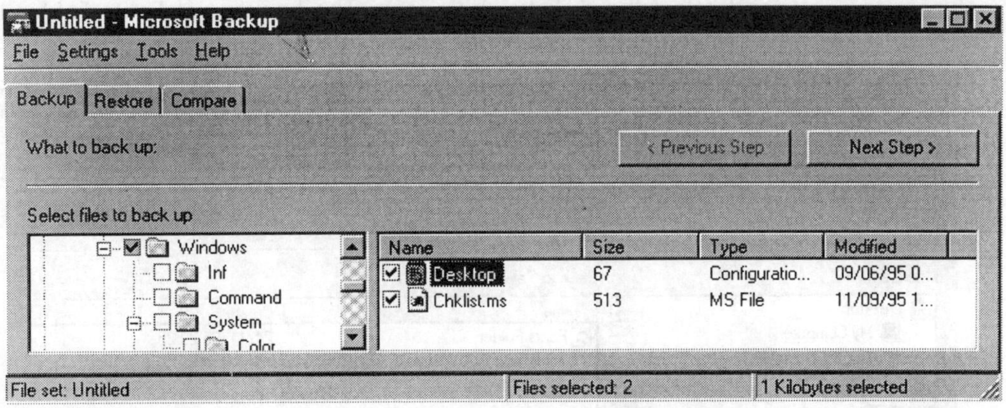

Figure 5

Incremental backup skips files that have not changed since their last backup, eg files such as system and program files are read only and will not change as data files do.

Verify backup... Select this option and Backup will check that the backed up files are the same as the originals.

Use data compression... Select this option – the backed up files will be compressed on the diskette, saving disk space.

..... tape backups Leave these two options unselected as they only apply to tape backups.

Always erase on floppy disk backups. Do not select this option unless you want the files on practice diskette b to be erased. It is a useful command when using old diskettes for backup.

Click the **OK** button.

9. **Running and saving the backup.** Click the **Start Backup** button. A dialogue box appears asking you to name the backup set. (you can save the backup instructions as a named file that can be run whenever you want to backup the same set of files again)

   Enter the file name **Fonts Folder** in the **Backup Set** box and click the **OK** button.
   Do not enter a password.

   The backup operation starts, a message box showing you its progress.
   This is followed immediately by the compare operation specified in section 8 – the backup copies are checked against the originals.
   Finally you are returned to the Backup window.

10. **Restoring from a backup.** If all goes well you may never need to use your backup. This section examines the various options.

   Click the **Restore** tab in the Backup window. The list of drives etc to restore from are displayed in the left hand window.
   Make sure that your backup disk, practice disk b is still in the drive and select the diskette drive icon. The backup set **Fonts Folder** is displayed in the right hand window – see Figure 6.

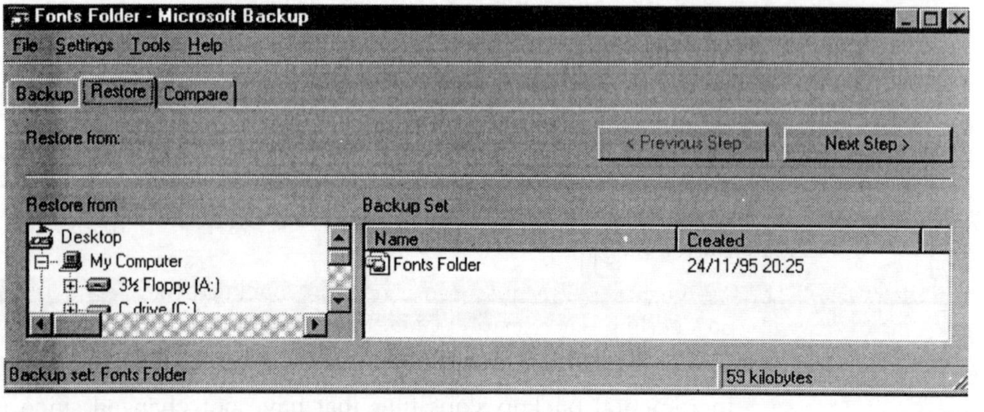

Figure 6

Click the **Next Step** button.

Keep clicking the icon and the backed up files are displayed – see Figure 7.

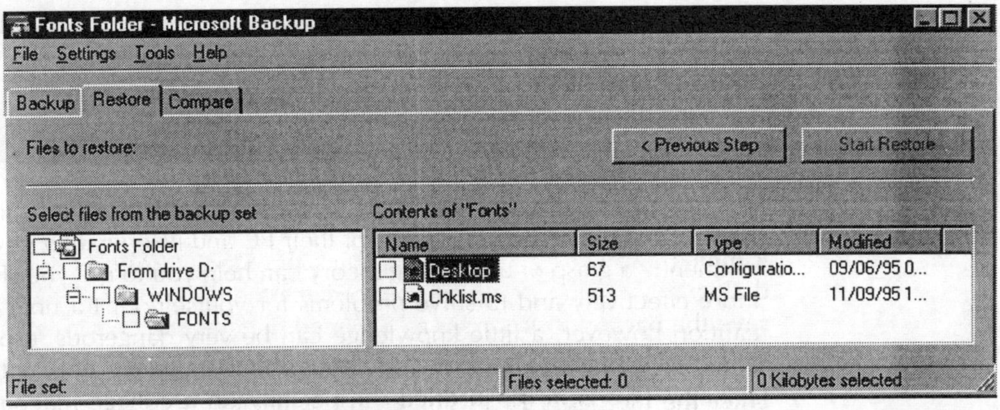

Figure 7

11. **Restore options.** You now have the option to restore all the files or select certain ones.

    Open the **Settings** menu and **Options.**

    Click the **Restore** tab.

    The dialogue box offers various options, let's review them:

    Location options. These three options allow you to restore the files to their original locations. This is the usual option when you are restoring to the same computer.
    The alternate locations options may be useful if you are restoring files to another computer with a different directory structure. (the Compare tab allows you to compare restored files in different locations with the backups)

    Verify option checks that the restored files are the same as the backups.

    Overwrite options you can choose whether any files with the same name are automatically overwritten, or only older versions with the same name. You can also set Restore to prompt you when this happens. This option is important when files may have changed since they were backed up and you do not wish to restore an earlier version.

12. As we have only just performed the backup there is no point in proceeding with Restore. Click the **Cancel** button and exit Backup.

13. You may wonder where backup set **Fonts Folder** is stored.

    Open **Explorer** and then open the drive containing the Windows folder.
    It contains the **Program Files** folder – open this and finally open the **Accessories** folder. You will see that it is stored there.

    If desired you could create a shortcut to this backup file – see Unit 7.

14. **Independent activity.** Providing you have the authority to copy files to the hard disk back up the files in the Accounts Folder on practice disk a to hard disk.
Save the backup set as a file and then restore them.

Note – Checking and Managing Your System.

The next few activities aimed at users who want to understand more about the technical aspects of their PC and its operating environment – a grasp of underlying theory can help you to use your PC more effectively and to solve problems for yourself. First a note of caution however, a little knowledge can be very dangerous, especially if it leads to casual and thoughtless tinkering with vital settings. This is never justified – especially on a college machine that is shared with others! In many of these exercises therefore, you will be observing and finding out about your system rather than changing it.

Activity 2 Checking a disk

1. Open the **My Computer** application and right click the icon for your PC's hard disk, eg C or D drive.

   Select **Properties** from the menu that appears.

2. The Properties dialogue box opens, make sure that the General tab is selected.
   The window shows the total capacity of the hard disk and the amount of free and used space. You can also label the hard disk, something that is normally done when the disk is first formatted – see Unit 3, Activity 1.

   Click the **Cancel** button.

3. Insert practice diskette b, right click the diskette drive icon and open the Properties dialogue box again.

   Check the amount of free disk space.

   Click the **Tools** tab – three disk utilities are offered. Click the Help (?) button, top right of the window and find out what each does:

   Error-checking status. This uses the ScanDisk utility to check for and repair errors. It can detect sectors (parts of tracks) on the disk surface that are bad or about to fail and mark them so they are not used. This should be done periodically, especially when disks get older. ScanDisk cannot check networked or CD-ROM drives

   Backup status. We have already used backup in Activity 1.

   Defragmentation status. As old files are deleted they leave scattered spaces free on disk. A new file may be fitted into a number of these spaces, ie fragmented, rather than as one contiguous block. Such files take longer to retrieve from disk, and need defragmenting to reorganise them, especially when data is being added and deleted frequently. The Defragmenter moves files around on the disk until all the parts of a file are stored next to each other. This should be done regularly on hard drives.

4. **Using ScanDisk.** Click the **Check Now** button. A dialogue box appears – see Figure 8.

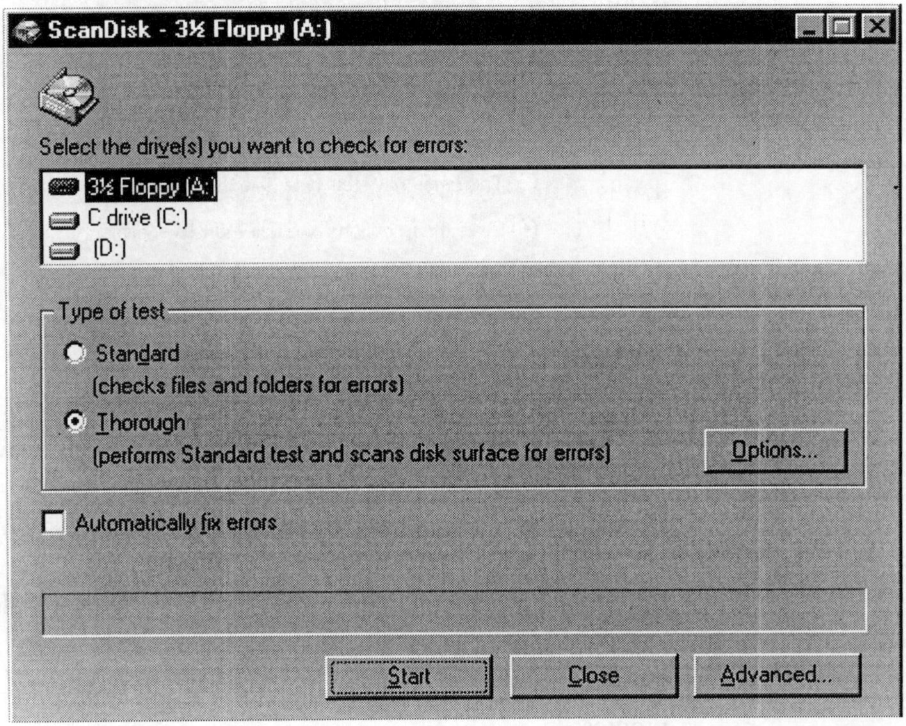

Figure 8

Make sure the diskette icon is selected, and select the **Thorough** option which checks the disk surface as well as files and folders.

Click the **Start** button.
The diskette is checked for errors – a slow process. If ScanDisk detects an error you will be asked if you want it fixed. Click **Yes.**
Eventually a results window shows the number of bad sectors (if any) and other disk information.

Close the ScanDisk window.

5. **Defragmenting a disk.** Assuming that the Tools tab is still selected in the Properties window click the **Defragment Now..** button.
A dialogue box appears, perhaps telling you that your disk does not need defragmenting.

Click the **Select Drive** button. Select the diskette drive then **OK.**

Click the **Advanced** button. A further dialogue box appears – see Figure 9.

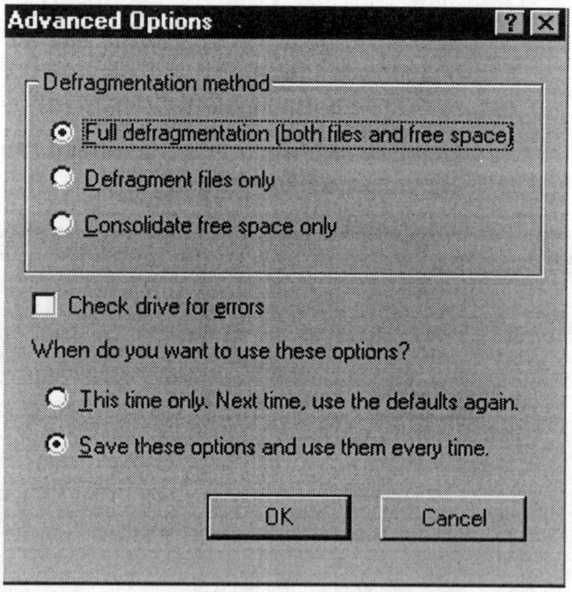

Figure 9

You can opt to defragment files, free space or both; leave the first option (full defragmentation) selected.

Deselect the option **Check drive for errors** if necessary. (we have already done this using ScanDisk)

Click **OK** – you are returned to the Disk Defragmenter dialogue box.

Click the **Start** button.

Click the **Show Details** button to see the defragmentation in progress.

Click the **Legend** button for an explanation of the defragment screen.

Exit from the Defragmenter and close the Properties dialogue box..

Activity 3 Compressing disks using Drivespace

You can create more space on hard drives and diskettes using the Windows 95 DriveSpace utility. You can create up to double the available disk space in many cases.

This is achieved by compressing the disk. You can compress an entire drive (including existing files), the free space or part of a drive. The compressed files are only readable on a PC with Windows 95 or MS-DOS DoubleSpace. However a compressed disk can be decompressed if you need to use it on a PC that does not have Windows 95.

When a drive is compressed another drive letter is assigned to the disk, eg drive C becomes drive H. Part of the drive remains uncompressed and is called the *host drive,* (H) the remainder of the drive is compressed into a single file – *a compressed volume file* or CVF (C).

Normally the host drive remains hidden from the user unless it contains more than 2MB of free space, in which case it is visible using Explorer or My Computer. Diskettes can also be compressed in a similar way.

Note: Read this before trying this activity!

Unless you are running short of disk space you may not need to use DriveSpace. Once you have used DriveSpace you must continue to use Windows 95 or MS-DOS DoubleSpace in order to access the compressed drive – the Windows Uninstall utility is disabled. This applies even to diskettes. So if you are sharing a PC with others you may decide not to go ahead with this activity, or stop at section 5.

1. Insert practice disk b in the diskette drive.

Click the **Start** button and select **Programs** then **Accessories** and finally **Systems Tools.**

Select DriveSpace.

2. Select the diskette drive from the window that appears.

Open the Drive menu and select **Compress.** A dialogue box appears showing the estimated compression gains.

Click the **Options** button.

3. The Compression Options dialogue box appears offering three options:

Drive letter of host drive The default is H – you can change it if this letter has been used or will be used for another drive. If so choose another letter.

Free space on host drive Leave this set at 0.00. You can choose to leave part of the disk uncompressed, normally because certain programs will not run on compressed drives. You would need to adjust the free space to hold these programs.

Hide host drive This option is only active if you have more than 2Mb of free disk space – not possible on a diskette.

Click the **OK** button to return to the main dialogue box and click the **Start** button.

4. A message box informs you that compression may take some time and offers you the option of backing up files. This is a wise precaution, although compression is very reliable you need to guard against accidents. You may also need uncompressed copies to use on a PC without the DriveSpace utility. However we already have copies of the files on practice disk a so we may safely skip this precaution in this instance.

Click the **Compress Now** button.

5. If you get the message:

   If you continue you will no longer be able to uninstall Windows 95

   Do you want to continue?

   Click the **No** button, read the note at the start of this activity and consider your options!

6. When compression is complete a dialogue box displays the compression statistics.

   Return to the **DriveSpace** window for the compressed drive.

   Exit to the **My Computer** window. The new drive is not visible in the My Computer window as the host drive is less than 2Mb.

7. **Uncompressing drives**. You may decide to uncompress a drive, eg a diskette may need to be decompressed to use it in another PC.

   Select the drive in the DriveSpace Window.

   Open the **Drive** menu and select **Uncompress.**
   A dialogue box shows you the space available after the disk is uncompressed.

   Click the **Start** button.

8. **Information only. Adjusting free space.** If you need more uncompressed space on disk – see section 3 – open the Drive menu and select Adjust Free Space.

9. Exit DriveSpace.

Activity 4 Checking your system

Introduction

The System option in the Control Panel provides technical information and diagnostics about all aspects of your system, including the hardware. Some are too technical for a publication of this type but others can be used to provide useful supplementary information such as the type of central processing unit, hard disk types and memory.

1. Click the **Start** button and select the **Settings** then the **Control Panel** option.

   Double click the **System** icon.
   The System Properties window appears displaying general information about your PC including the processor type – 486, Pentium etc, and the amount of RAM or main memory in Mb.

2. Click the **Performance** tab. Various information is given on your PC's performance. If you are unclear about the meaning of a tech-

nical term click the help button (?) at the top right of the dialogue box then click the term itself.

Windows 95 configures your PC for optimum usage; for this reason there is normally no need to use the Advanced settings at the bottom of the dialogue box. There may be a window displaying additional information if your PC is not set up for optimum performance.

3. Click the **Device Manager** tab. A dialogue box appears. Device Manager allows you to check and change the devices connected to your system.

   Pictured in the window are a list of devices on your system, see, eg, Figure 10.

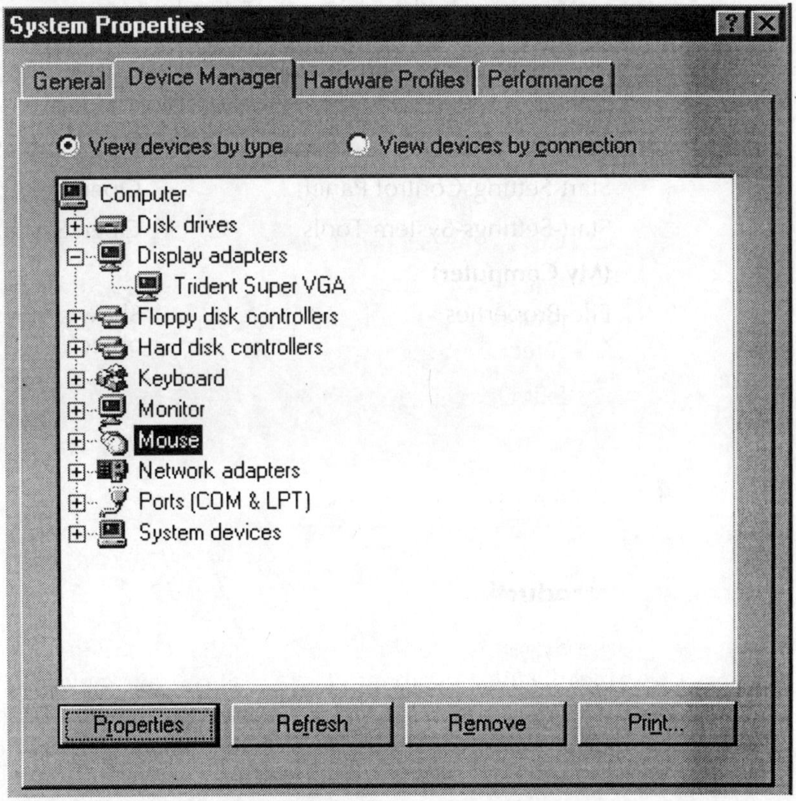

Figure 10

   To expand the information click the '+' sign next to the device. All the devices of that type (often only one) are shown.

   Double click on a device type to find out more about it.

4. Click the '+' sign next to **System devices.** A list appears.
   If a device is marked with an exclamation mark this indicates a problem.

Double click on some of these devices to find out more about them. Often the only information is that the device is working correctly.

Click the '-' sign to close the system devices list.

5. Exit from the System Properties dialogue box and close the Control Panel.

Summary of menu commands

Notes

Menu commands show the menu name first, followed by the command to choose from the menu, e.g. Edit-Clear means open the Edit menu and select the Clear command. Where a command is available from a particular window this is indicated in brackets.

Start-Programs-Accessories-System Tool-DriveSpace	Open DriveSpace
Start-SettingsControl Panel	Open the Control Panel
Start-Settings-System Tools	Open System Tools
(My Computer)	
File-Properties	Show properties of selected object

Index